Villages Around Maidenhead

VILLAGES AROUND MAIDENHEAD

LUKE OVER

First published 2009

The History Press
The Mill, Brimscombe Port
Stroud, Gloucestershire, GL5 2QG
www.thehistorypress.co.uk

British Library Cataloguing in Publication Data.
A catalogue record for this book is available from the British Library.

ISBN 978 0 7524 5289 0

Typesetting and origination by The History Press
Printed in Great Britain

Contents

	Acknowledgements	6
	Foreword	7
	Introduction – The Domesday Legacy	9
1	The Domesday Villages	15
2	Cookham	21
3	Bray	39
4	Oakley – Vampires and Monkeys	55
5	Waltham and Shottesbrooke	69
6	Thicket and Stubbings	87
7	Hurley	95
8	Taplow	101
9	The Hundred of Desborough	111
10	Binfield and Wargrave	121

Acknowledgements

The author wishes to thank the following:

Fran Edwards and the friends of Maidenhead Heritage Centre for the reproduction of the text.

Richard Poad, Chairman of the Maidenhead Heritage Trust for writing the Foreword.

Artist Chris Tyrrell for allowing me to reproduce two of his illustrations on the covers of the book.

And the *Maidenhead Advertiser* and Maidenhead Library for their help and encouragement in the past.

Cover illustrations:

Front: Shotttesbrooke Park House and Church. (by kind permission of Lady Christian Smith)

Back: The Saxon Palace at Old Windsor, *c.* 1060.

Foreword

Luke Over MBE is the pre-eminent historian of the Maidenhead area. His many books and newspaper articles have helped excite people about the amazingly varied history of this part of the Royal County of Berkshire.

In this new book, bringing together a large collection of articles originally written for the *Maidenhead Advertiser*, Luke takes his reader on a wide-ranging journey through the lovely villages which encircle Maidenhead. Their fascinating story spans the ages; from Stone Age hand-axes to twentieth century helicopters. There is ample demonstration of Luke's encyclopaedic knowledge on every page.

Luke has been an enthusiastic and long-standing supporter of Maidenhead Heritage Centre, which is now well established as the local museum for the Maidenhead area. We are extremely grateful to him for allowing us to publish this book, which will directly contribute towards the Heritage Centre's future development. Our visitors can explore local history through our exhibitions, photographs, talks and website. We are proud to be continuing the work which Luke began.

Richard Poad MBE
Chairman
Maidenhead Heritage Centre
www.maidenheadheritage.org.uk
September 2009

Introduction

The Domesday Legacy

Although the Great Domesday survey of 1086 predominantly provides information on the early Norman settlements in East Berkshire, it also gives us some insight into the manors existing in the late Anglo-Saxon period before the Conquest of 1066. Certainly in the case of the area in question, there were no manors added or subtracted when the new owners took over, although in some instances they increased or decreased in size.

To some extent, the manors appeared to have developed from the earlier Romano-British estates, but it was some time before the Saxons had any sort of stable organisation. The first mention of a shire was in the year AD 860, when Berkshire took its name from a wood (or Berroc). East Berkshire may have been heavily wooded at this time, which would account for the sparse settlement of the area. Early Saxon charters seem to indicate a pattern of enclosures and clearings within a wooded area.

Most evidence of the early Saxon period in East Berkshire can only be gleaned from the *Anglo-Saxon Chronicles* or from the results of excavations. Reading was styled a 'royal vill' in AD 870, and was taken in mid-winter AD 871 by the heathen army of Danes. The Danish hosts fortified the town by throwing up works in a narrow strip of land between the Thames and the Kennet. King Ethelred and his brother forced their way to the gate of the town, but were driven back to Wiscelet (Whistley) and over the Loddon at Twyford.

Excavations at Old Windsor showed that there was a settlement there by AD 750. In the ninth century there was a considerable amount of building on the site which was probably the royal residence, and later the palace of Edward the Confessor. At this time a water mill with three vertical wheels was erected, with at least 1,100m in length dug across a loop in the Thames. Wooden buildings from the tenth and eleventh centuries were found in the upper levels, and a destruction period in the twelfth century probably equates with the abandonment of the old palace prior to its replacement as a residence by Windsor Castle, built in 1070.

Bray was an important manor in Saxon times, but there is little documentary evidence. Excavations have brought to light a seventh-century site of Moor Farm, Holyport, and a fifth-century occupation near Bray Marina. More is known

King Edward the Confessor (from the Bayeux Tapestry).

of Cookham, which was a frontier town on the borders of Wessex and Mercia. The Burghal Hideage of AD 914-18 mentions the fort of Sceaftsege, which has been identified as being located on Sashes Island. A document of AD 798 records that there was a monastery there by AD 750, and another records the meeting of Witan with King Ethelred in AD 997, which could indicate the site of a royal palace. Excavations have revealed Saxon warrior barrows at Rowborough and on Cockmarsh.

By the ninth century, Sonning was an important ecclesiastical centre and the site of an Episcopal residence. Of the other settlements in East Berkshire we have very little evidence, but most have Saxon names. The suffixes '-ham' (e.g. Waltham, Remenham) and '-ing' (e.g. Reading, Sonning) together with '-field', '-hurst' and '-worth' are typically Saxon, and apply to most of the later manors.

In 1066 the last of the great Saxon Kings, Edward the Confessor, died, leaving his throne to the Earl Harold, who reigned for only four months before perishing at the Battle of Hastings. The victor, William the Conqueror, the first of the Norman Kings, was to change the face of East Berkshire, and record forever its settlements in the *Domesday Book* of 1086.

Although William seized the Crown in battle, in truth he had a valid claim as Edward the Confessor, who was childless, had made William his heir as early as 1051,

King William the Conqueror (from the Bayeux Tapestry).

despite opposition from Godwine, Earl of Wessex, and later from his successor, the Earl Harold. At a later date Harold promised to support William's claim, but on the death of Edward, in January 1066, he had a change of heart and accepted the throne. He was only King for a few months, before he was killed.

The Duke of Normandy established himself as King William I of England. By 1070 he had reorganised the country and replaced many of the surviving Saxon landowners with his own Norman knights. This interchange of ownership eventually led to confusion as to who owned what, and William, dependent on the taxes collected from the manors, was determined to put the matter right. Accordingly he called together his councillors at Christmas 1085 and held discussions with them in the Chapter House at Gloucester Abbey.

At the meeting William laid down his plans for the Great Survey of England, which when completed was to become the *Domesday Book*. He asked his barons and churchmen to prepare lists of their landholdings, together with information on resources and manpower. The barons in turn instructed their reeves and bailiffs to provide the required information on each of their estates. The information was handed in to the shire or county courts and was collected by Domesday Commissioners, specially appointed by the sheriff of each shire.

The details of the Survey were written down in abbreviated Latin by monks and priests and a fair copy was made by the Exchequer officials at Winchester, and probably Bury St Edmunds. The Commissioners travelled on seven circuits to gather the information, and that of the Eastern circuit, notably Essex, Suffolk and Norfolk, was bound together to make Volume XI of the *Domesday Book*, which was 451 pages long. Most of the other counties, or shires, appear in Volume I which is 382 pages, but in a larger format. Each shire summary was inscribed in a quire, or small booklet, with forty-four lines of script to each folio. The initial survey was completed extremely quickly considering the size of the undertaking and the results were handed to William on 1 August 1086 at Old Sarum, just outside Salisbury.

The first transcript of the survey was called a 'descriptio', or 'writing down'. It was then called the *Book of Winchester* and kept in the Treasury there. By 1170 it had become known as the *Domesday Book*, and a legal bible used frequently to settle disputes over the title of land. The word 'Domesday' translated as the 'Day of Judgement', against which there was no appeal. It was still being used in the nineteenth century to settle disputes. Today, the unique document survives intact and is being housed and cared for by the Public Record Office.

Apart from the natural curiosity of William as to the extent of his landholdings, his reasons for compiling the *Domesday Book* were political, feudal, judicial and, above all, financial. Professor Maitland described it as a 'gold book' and a document from which the King could calculate the annual taxes owed to him by his tenants. The name originated from the tenth century when the English Kings collected substantial amounts of silver in taxes to buy off marauding Danish armies. This was known as Danegeld.

The entries in the *Domesday Book* tended to follow a similar format throughout. As today the country was divided into counties or shires, each under the administration of a sheriff or 'Shire Reeve'. Shires were subdivided into 'hundreds', which were notionally areas of 100 hides, but tended not to be that accurate. One hide was roughly equal to 120 acres. Within each hundred were the Domesday manors or settlements, and the boroughs, which roughly equate with modern towns.

The meaning of the word 'manor' in the Domesday context should be clearly understood. It is a much misunderstood word and is usually associated with a large country house. Its true meaning is that of a 'working agricultural unit', similar to the modern-day farm and the preceding Romano-British villa. Sometimes a natural progression can be traced, and a local example is perhaps Feens Farm, Littlewick, which originally started as a villa site, and progressed to the medieval manor of Fiennes. A Domesday manor comprised arable land and pasture and woodland for animals, with perhaps a few humble dwellings and a mill. Principal manors were more like villages, with several houses, a church and a manor house where the bailiff or even the tenant himself resided. The manorial names listed in the *Domesday Book* may only be the principal sites, with other dependent settlements not mentioned.

All land at Domesday belonged to the King, although the records show that the Crown held 17 per cent 'in lordship'. The bishops and abbots held 26 per cent and the balance was in the hands of the King's tenants-in-chief. Most landholders were from northern France, but there were still some Anglo-Saxons and Danes. All entries show the ownership before 1066, in the time of King Edward, and this changed rapidly about 1070 when King William rewarded his knights for their support.

The Domesday Commissioners were evidently instructed to assign a set value to each resource within a manor, and this so-called value was an estimate of the total the lord would receive annually in money or kind from his peasants. These payments in kind would include such things as the annual dues paid by a mill, a proportion of the eels caught in a fishery, and the pigs kept in woodlands. The geld or tax assessment was based on the figures expressed in hides (120 acres). Therefore, a manor assessed at forty hides would pay the current rate of so many shillings per hide in a similar way to modern rateable values.

Life on the manor centred around the hall where the court was held. The landowner would not necessarily be present very often and the administration of the estate would be carried out by the reeve, whilst the priest would deal with any spiritual requirements. The workers on the land were tied to their manor, but most had a small stake in its resources. They rendered services to the lord, and ploughed his lands as well as their own. The Survey records many classes of peasants, the highest in rank being the freemen or sokemen. In order of hierarchy, the Berkshire entries names villeins (villagers), bordars (smallholders) and cottars (cottagers) and, last of all, serfs or slaves, who were enforced workers. As regards to estimating the population of a manor, the book only records the head of households, and to calculate the true number of bodies

Ockwells Manor, Maidenhead.

a multiplication factor of four is often used. Slaves are normally counted as individuals, whilst retainers in castles and monks and nuns were not counted at all.

Land recorded at Domesday comprised 35 per cent arable, 25 per cent pasture and meadow, 15 per cent woodland and 25 per cent marginal land and waste. With few material possessions, the total economy of the manor was dependent on the correct usage of land for the production of crops and livestock. Most important was the arable land, which was divided into plough lands and used to grow wheat, barley, oats and beans. The figure given for the actual number of ploughs was a good guide to the agricultural capacity of the manor, although the actual acreage cultivated annually by one plough is not known with accuracy. A plough team consisted of eight oxen. Smaller gardens were used to grow cabbages, leeks, onions, peas and herbs and, in some cases, the settlements had vineyards.

Some flour from the grain was ground by hand, but the bulk in water-powered mills. Windmills were not built until the twelfth century. In most cases, water power was available from rivers or streams, but with land-bound manors arrangements could be made for milling to be done in neighbouring settlements.

Pasture and meadow, usually expressed in acres, were important for grazing and the rearing of livestock. Sheep were of great economic importance, providing wool for garments as well as meat. There were cows for milking, oxen for working, and horses for transport. Pigs were an important source of meat and these were fed on acorns and beech mast in surrounding woodland. With Berkshire, numbers of animals tend not to be mentioned, although woodlands are measured by the number of pigs they could support. Apart from pasturing swine, woodlands provided a source of timber and brushwood. Royal forests, however, were restricted from any further use, and were stocked with deer and wild boar specifically for the King's hunting parties.

In some cases, bees are mentioned. These provided honey and wax, and were measured in units of hives. More important, perhaps, were the fisheries which were located in most streams and rivers. These provided another source of food and were usually valued in eels. Eel traps were in use well into the nineteenth century.

The mention of churches in the *Domesday Book* is only incidental, and is generally due to the existence of taxable glebe land. The omission of a church does not necessarily mean that one did not exist, but merely that it had no relevance for tax purposes. In some cases early charters tell us of the churches which existed in 1086, and where abbeys and priories held the land there was almost certainly a place of worship in the relevant manor.

William the Conqueror died in September 1087, one year after the Survey was completed. The chronicles record that it was a year of great famine, severe storms, and plague epidemics which greatly reduced the population accounted for in the *Domesday Book*.

Chapter One

The Domesday Villages

A possible Domesday Road ran from Windsor to Reading along the line of the present B3024. The road skirted the bounds of Windsor Forest and the early manors mentioned in the *Domesday Book* seems to be situated close to this highway. Those that are not are instead on the bank of the Thames, and took advantage of the river to boost their economy and provide an additional means of communication.

Saxon charters show that the settlements of White Waltham, Waltham St Lawrence and Shottesbrooke were at one time a single estate, but by 1066 they had been separated. There are two entries in the book for White Waltham. The first, which was called Waltham at Domesday, was an area assessed at ten hides (1,200 acres) and was held by Chertsey Abbey for the purpose of providing household supplies for the monks. This can be identified as an area around the present church and village with arable land for ten ploughs. This was later to become the manor of Berry or Bury and the name still persists in Bury Court Farm. The entry mentions a small church which was the predecessor of the present building.

The second entry for White Waltham was a settlement called Waltha which had its centre at Woodlands Park and took in land as far away as Littlewick Green. It was in the possession of the Bishop of Durham in 1066, and before had belonged to the Earl Harold who perished at the Battle of Hastings. The sub-tenancy was in the hands of the Abbey at Waltham Cross, from whom the later village took its name. In the thirteenth century it became the manor of Heywoods, which is thought to be a corruption of Harolds Wood. The outlying area of Littlewick became the manor of Fiennes or Woolley, which still exist in the names Woolley Hall and Feens Farm.

Waltham St Lawrence was held by the King and was part of the royal estate. Before 1066 it was the property of Queen Edith, consort to Edward the Confessor. Being in royal hands meant that it was exempt from paying tax. It had a population of 148, which was quite considerable in the eleventh century. No church is mentioned in the entry, but we know that one existed as it is mentioned in the Hurley charter. The location of the Domesday village is not apparent but it may have been in the nearby Burringham Wood, a name made up of the three Saxon components; 'Burh' (a fortified place) and '-ing' and '-ham', both suffixes that indicate a settlement. The manors of Beenham and Billingbear evolved in this parish during the thirteenth century.

Shottesbrooke was held from the King by Alfward the Goldsmith, and had been held in Saxon times by his father. Part of the economy of the manor was based on charcoal burning, the resultant product being used in the manufacture of precious metal regalia for the King's court. It was still making charcoal in 1166 when a Pipe Roll records the settlement as 'Sotesbrook Aurifaborum'.

A church is mentioned at Domesday, and the foundations lay beneath the present church which was built in 1337 by Sir William Trussell, who at the same time founded a college there for a warden, five chaplains and two clerks. The population was about 106 in 1066 and this diminished later, giving Shottesbrooke the status of a deserted medieval village. Aerial photographs reveal the old village in Shottesbrooke Park, which was probably deserted at the time the area was emparked.

The woodland settlements mentioned so far, which were formed by the clearance of land by assarting, had an economy mainly based on agriculture and animal husbandry. In the woods, pigs could be reared on acorns and beech mast, but there was little meadow for grazing. These can be contrasted with the settlements situated on the River Thames, which had large areas of water meadow together with water mills and fisheries to help boost their economy. If we regard each manor as a separate unit, it is clear that some trading between settlements was necessary for all to survive. The milling of flour is a good example. The Thameside manors with mills probably ground the cereals for the woodland manors, who would perhaps reciprocate by providing additional pork in exchange. Windmills, of course, had not been invented in the eleventh century.

The first of the Thameside manors was that of Bray, a royal manor assessed at eighteen hides, standing within its own hundred. It was exempt from paying tax and had twenty-nine ploughs, a large area of arable land. It also had a woodland for 100 pigs and eleven acres of meadow. It differed from other Thames manors in that it had no mills and fisheries. This peculiarity might suggest that the Domesday settlement was situated away from the river. With less river management, the flat plain from Cookham to Bray would have been subject to regular flooding, a fact that is emphasised when one considers that both of these villages have raised causeways. Also, Maidenhead town, although built at a later date, was sited half a mile from the river, probably for the same reason.

Bray is unusual in that it was the only manor in Berkshire to boast three men-at-arms. These were knights living in the manor, maybe at Holyport, because of its proximity to Windsor Castle. When required they would be expected to fight for the King and provide soldiers on the basis of one man for each five hide unit. A church with sixty acres of land attached is mentioned, and this would have predated the present church building by at least 200 years. The Bray entry also records that 'Reinbald the priest holds one hide which belongs to the church'. Reinbald was chancellor to the King and Abbot of Cirencester, and probably held the church at Bray as rector. The land in question was at Braywick and was styled in 1133 as the Rectorial manor of Canon Hill.

Holyport, having a Saxon foundation, was undoubtedly there at Domesday as part of the manor of Bray. It was separated from Bray by the Shaffelmoor, a large area of swamp which ran from the Thames to Ockwells Manor, and which was drained in the eighteenth century by the provision of the Cut. The suffix '-port' denotes that Holyport was probably a market centre on the Domesday Road, ideally situated at a short distance from a number of settlements. This theory is perhaps borne out of the fact that in the thirteenth century there were six manor houses within half a mile of Holyport. Bray as a whole had thirteen manors formed by subinfeudation in the medieval period, an abnormally high number by any standard. The manor houses were probably convenient residences for noblemen who needed to live close to Windsor Castle and the market centre, and ancient documents show that the landholdings associated with these manors were often located in a different part of the county.

A second entry in the *Domesday Book* records a separate settlement of Bras, which is located in the neighbouring hundred of Beynhurst. The similarity of the name has suggested to past historians that it might be a duplicate entry for Bray, but I think this is unlikely. It was a small manor of two hides held by Alwin, son of Chipping, with a population of forty and a church. The latter aspect is most puzzling as it does not tie in with any other church in the area which has a medieval foundation. The most likely candidate for its location is Touchen End, anciently called Twychene, which was a bailiwick of the manor of Woolley or Fiennes at Littlewick. A free chapel of Woolley is mentioned in 1351 which might link in with the church at the settlement of Bras.

Cookham was another major settlement of twenty hides held by the King and exempt from tax. It had two mills, two fisheries and fifty acres of meadow which probably equate with Widbrook and Cockmarsh. The entry shows that it had a 'new market', presumably set up by William I and probably located on the edge of the moor. The manor had a church, which was again held from the King in alms by Reinbald the Priest. This area can be identified as Canon Court, north of Furze Platt, and like Reinbald's holding in Bray, belonged to the Abbey of Cirencester. For many hundreds of years the abbot retained the right of free pasturage for cattle at Widbrook and hogs at Cockmarsh.

The land held by Reinbald later became the manor of Canons and was one of the eight Cookham manors formed by subinfeudation. The most important manor was probably Lullebrook, which was granted in 1205 to Adam de Burnham. Others include Bradleys and Babham End and the later manor of Bullocks located at White Place Farm. Ancient cottages situated at the farm date back to Elizabethan times.

In the Saxon period, and as early as the eighth century, Cookham had been an important frontier town on the border of Wessex and Mercia. Documents record an ancient monastery there and a meeting of the King's Parliament in AD 997. Many Saxon burials have been excavated at Cookham, and the Burghal Hideage records the site of King Alfred's fort of Sceaftsege on Sashes Island. Evidence suggests that the Saxon settlement may have first been located at Cookham Rise, away from the area liable to flood.

At Domesday, Bisham was held by the tenant-in-chief, Henry de Ferrers. The entry shows that the manor has twelve arpents of vines, which is unusual in Berkshire. The introduction of vines to England is usually associated with French monks, but it was not until the reign of King Stephen (1135–54) that the manor was granted in free alms to the Knights Templars, who established a preceptory there. The preceptory

Bisham Abbey.

forms the basis of the present Bisham Abbey, although a later house of Austin Canons, founded in 1337, was abolished. Bisham had a church at Domesday, but the tower of the present All Saints appears to date to 1150, and is a good example of Norman architecture.

Part of the Church of St Mary's, Hurley, may well have been standing in 1086. The excavations carried out by Rivers-Moore in the 1930s seem to indicate that it may have been an integral part of the priory. The Domesday entry mentions the existence of a church but not the priory, although we know from the foundation charter that the religious house was *in situ* by September 1087, as it was signed by William the Conqueror before his death. The fact that the priory was omitted from the Domesday survey does not, however, mean it did not exist, but merely that it was not liable for tax. A good example is the powerful Abingdon Abbey, which is not mentioned but held lands all over the county.

The priory was founded by the tenant-in-chief, Geoffrey de Mandeville, Earl of Essex, as a cell of St Peter's Westminster in memory of his wife. It held the patronage of the Church of Waltham St Lawrence and the chapels of Warfield and Remenham, two of which are also omitted from the Domesday Survey.

As a settlement, Hurley was assessed at fourteen hides and had other land for eighteen ploughs. Its population can be estimated at 158 peasants, plus any monks if they existed. It also had a mill and two fisheries. Although the manor was dominated

The Norman church at Bisham.

Elizabethan cottages at White Place Farm, Cookham.

by the priory who held most of the land, a later manor seems to have developed at Hall Place which was held by John de Hurley in 1220.

Finally, Wargrave was, for the most part, a royal manor which passed back and forth between the Crown and the Bishops of Winchester. In the tenth century it had been granted to Queen Emma, the wife of Ethelred, who gave it to the Old Minster at Winchester. It reverted to William I at Domesday and was passed on to the other Norman Kings until 1150 when it was given back to Winchester by Stephen. It was reclaimed by Henry II and reverted to Winchester in 1218. By this time the manor was in Windsor Forest and the bishop had obtained exclusive hunting rights.

The ancient manor of Wargrave seems to have been centred around Mill Green, which takes its name from a mill that stood upon a stream leading to the River Loddon. During the medieval period there were at least five new manors in Wargrave. The most important of these was Ruscombe, which was mentioned as early as 1091 as Rothescamp in the foundation charter of the cathedral at Old Sarum, when ten hides was granted by Osmund, the reigning bishop. The present Church of St James dates back to the late twelfth century and was the subject of a famous visitation in 1220 when it was held by the vicarage of Sonning. At this time the building was found to be in ruinous condition and the chaplain totally incompetent.

Chapter Two

Cookham

Cookham came into existence in Anglo-Saxon times, but fate seems to have decreed that the site of the first village will remain a mystery. Excavations carried out during the last 100 years have failed to produce any material evidence of its existence, and this has puzzled many historians. However, documentary evidence indicates that Saxon Cookham was an important stronghold on the border of Mercia and Wessex, with a fort built by King Alfred to defend the Wessex frontier.

The *Domesday Book* of 1086 confirms the importance of Cookham, and records the area as part of the royal estate of Edward the Confessor. In 1066 it was twenty hides (2,400 acres) in size, similar to Windsor. It was valued at £50, while Windsor was £15 and Maidenhead a mere 60*s*. Cookham was eventually eclipsed by Maidenhead, a fast-growing town on the main road to Bristol and the west.

In Roman times the area where Cookham now stands would have been part of the estate of a villa-farm, and such a complex was located at Strand Castle in 1968. When the Romans left Britain, the Saxon raiders eventually conquered the country and formed their own settlements. The name Cookham is of Saxon origin ('Cook' is a tribal name; '-ham' a settlement) and the first village was probably in existence by AD 550. Pagan at first, the settlers were introduced to Christianity in the seventh century by Saint Birinus, a bishop from Dorchester-on-Thames. By AD 716 a charter records that a monastery had been built at Cookham and that Cynethryth, the widow of King Offa of Mercia, had been appointed abbess. Between this date and AD 798, the property passed between the Kings of Mercia and Wessex and was eventually given to the abbess, together with adjacent lands. At this time Cookham was officially part of Wessex, the Thames being the borderline between Wessex and Mercia.

The site of the monastery remains unknown, as indeed does the first settlement and no foundations have come to light in the present village. Indications are that the water level was higher in Saxon times and the area where the village now stands was a series of marshes and islands, only accessible by a causeway similar to that currently crossing Cookham Moor.

The first settlement may have been sited on higher ground at Cookham Rise, and local place names seem to indicate that this may be so. Before the houses were

King Ethelred holds court in Cookham, *c.* AD 996.

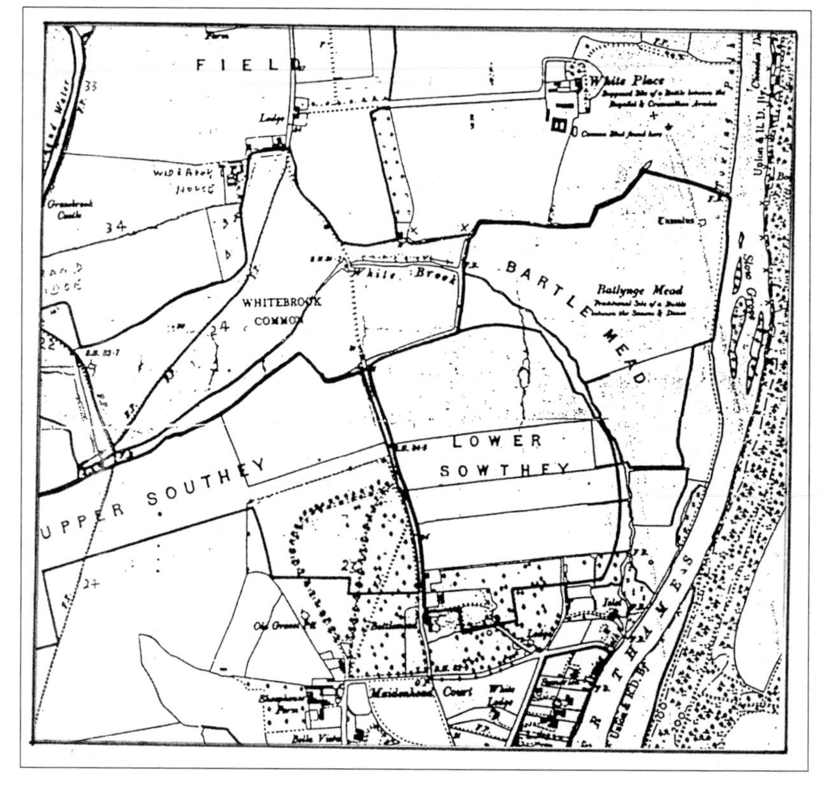

Field names at Widbrook Common, Cookham.

built, the area between Pinder Hall and the gasometers was taken up by two fields named Coxborrow and Ham Field. These may be interpreted as 'Cox' (Cook) '-burrow' (borough town) and 'Ham' (settlement) Field, and may well be the site of the earlier village. Next to Ham Field is an area that was known as Church Field. In the Domesday Survey it is recorded that Reinbald the Priest held 180 acres in Cookham, plus the church. A charter further records that the King granted Reinbald the church and all its lands, including Church Fields at Cannon Court. This surely infers that the first church was also built on higher ground and that the present church, which is suspected of having part of a Saxon wall around the sanctuary, had a later foundation date.

This settlement on the rise probably survived until the ninth century when it may have been destroyed by marauding Danes. Pushing their way upriver they eventually formed a stronghold at Reading in the years AD 870–71, but not without leaving their mark en route.

Battling Mead, south of Widbrook, is a reputed site of a battle between the Danes and the Saxons, and Danesfield Camp at Medmenham is also associated with the invaders. The name Odney (Odin's eye) may be named after the Danish god of war, but some believe it derives from the Saxon 'Oddanig' (Odda's Island).

In order to defend his territory against the Danes, Alfred the Great built a series of burhs, or forts, in Wessex before AD 900. These are listed in a document known as the Burghal Hideage, and include the fort of Sceaftesege, which was located on Sashes Island at Cookham. Bounded on three sides by the river, it would have been surrounded by a wooden palisade and commanded a good defensive position. The fort was allocated an area of 1,000 hides from which to draw men to defend the palisade, which means that the length of the palisade would have been 1,375 yards, calculated from the Burghal Hideage document. This in turn means that the fort enclosed about half of the fifty-four acres of the present island.

Material evidence for the existence of this fort is abundant. When the lock cut was made through Sashes Field in 1830, skeletons, swords and javelins were found. Dredging the cut in 1856 produced several more Danish weapons. In 1860, iron spearheads of a similar date were found in the river. In 1896 a winged axe was recovered, and in 1931 and 1958 barbed spearheads and human skeletons were unearthed on the island. Nearby, at Cookham Lock, wooden foundation piles were located in 1892, together with a horse's skeleton.

Elsewhere in Cookham there is much evidence of the hurried burial of warriors. In 1874 a burial mound was excavated on Cockmarsh and was found to contain the remains of a Saxon warrior, in the nature of a secondary interment. The skeleton was accompanied by a knife, a shield boss, some animal bones and a pottery drinking vessel, all articles to be used on the journey to another world. In 1864, twenty-seven human skeletons were found in a ballast pit at Cookham at an unknown location.

In the same year, during the construction of the railway from Maidenhead to High Wycombe, six burials were located on Rowborough Hill in a field known as 'Noah's Ark'. The grave goods comprised a sword, two spearheads, one dagger and three shield bosses, together with a two-handled basin in bronze. The site of this particular burial

Church of Holy Trinity, Cookham.

group raises an interesting point. In Frilford, Berkshire, a similar Saxon cemetery also occurs in a field known as 'Noah's Ark'. Is this merely a coincidence or is there some significance to the name? The word 'ark' can mean box or coffin in Anglo-Saxon. The mystery deepens when one considers the Saxon chieftain Sceaf, after whom the fort Sceaftsege was named. The *Abingdon Chronicles*, written in AD 977, record that Sceaf was the son of Noah and was born in Noah's Ark.

The site of the fort probably resulted in another settlement springing up on the flood plain where the present village now stands. The Saxon name Sutton, associated with a field and a road in Cookham, means 'South Town' and implies settlement to the north between there and the river. Such a settlement would require a new church, probably built on the site of the Norman building. This new town must have been considered important as it is recorded that in AD 997, King Ethelred the Unready held council in Cookham and that 'all the thegns [chieftains] gathered there from far and wide, both West Saxons and Mercians, Danes and English'.

Today Cookham is a picturesque Thameside village frequented by visitors during the summer months. It is perhaps difficult now to imagine its turbulent past and its importance as a strategically-placed frontier settlement in Anglo-Saxon times.

The place name of Cookham, which in the year AD 798 was spelt Coccham, indicates Anglo-Saxon origin. The location of the village indicates that it has always held a strategic position as a border town with the Thames dividing two separate kingdoms. Presently, the river separates Berkshire from Buckinghamshire, which in these untroubled times are linked by a bridge, first erected in 1840. In the distant

High Street, Cookham.

past however, neighbours were not so friendly and in the eighth century the village suffered from disputes between Mercia and Wessex. In Roman times too, Cookham was in the centre of the troubles between the Catavalauni and the Atrebates.

The key to the origins of Cookham lie in Sashes Island, near Cookham Lock, which today consists of fifty-four acres of peaceful grazing land. In the past, however, this stepping stone across the Thames has been the scene of many a skirmish and this fact has been supported by a mass of evidence. When the lock cut was put through the island in 1830, and in subsequent dredging activities, quantities of human skeletons associated with Roman, Saxon and Danish weapons have come to light. By the lock and at Hedsor Wharf, upright wooden piles and brushwood platforms have been located, suggesting substantial structures erected during the period of Roman and Saxon occupation. Unfortunately, when the lock cut was excavated the spoil was laid across the island to a depth of 4ft which has obliterated any surface indications of early activity.

It is likely that during the campaigns of AD 43-47 a Roman fort was situated on Sashes Island. The Camlet Way, a Roman road linking the cantonal capitals at St Albans and Silchester, south of Reading, has been traced from the north to Hedsor Wharf, where it crossed the river at the convenient bridging point at Sashes.

Recent research shows that where a Roman road crossed a river there was usually a small island port where heavy materials could be loaded and transported by water. An early map of Sashes, drawn in 1560, shows that there was a watercourse dividing the island which may well have originated as a Roman canal where boats could be

Wayfarers on Cookham Moor in the nineteenth century.

moored away from the main river current. This stream has since silted up but can still be traced on the island.

Such Roman forts always had an associated *vicus* or living settlement. An extension of the Camlet Way from Sashes shows that it crosses another Roman road at approximately the end of Whyteladyes Lane. Here, at the road junction, an extensive Roman settlement, situated just above the flood plain, was excavated in 1958 and again in 1968. Investigations showed that there was an occupation from the first to the fourth centuries with ditches, huts, a well and enclosure and several corn-drying kilns. This is the earliest indication of a major settlement at Cookham.

Saxon settlement in the Thames Valley began around AD 420, but little is known of this remote period. It would seem that at first, Cookham was in the territory of the Middle Saxons (Middlesex) until the early part of the seventh century when it was part of the Provincia of Sonning.

Evidence from place names seems to indicate that the first Saxon town of Cookham probably existed away from the flood plain at Coxborough in Cookham Rise. The adjoining Ham and Pound fields were probably the furthest extent of the settlement which would have comprised a series of wooden buildings with chalk foundations. This was undoubtedly the type of village that Saint Birinus would have visited when he began teaching Christianity to the West Saxons after he was appointed Bishop of Dorchester in AD 634. From this date until AD 726, the Cookham area was administered by the King of Wessex, after which it came under Aethelbald of Mercia. An existing charter of AD 798 records the earliest mention of a church in Cookham which was attached to a monastery in existence by the year AD 726. By AD 757, this

The floods at Cookham, 1894.

monastery had been given to the Archbishop of Canterbury by Athelbald, after which it fell into Wessex hands. However, it was retrieved by King Offa of Mercia when he defeated Cynewulf at the Battle of Benson in AD 779.

The charter of AD 798 records the transfer of the monastery to Offa's widow, the Abbess Cynethryth, in exchange for 220 hides of land in other parts of the country. As the whole of East Berkshire measures 218 hides, it is likely that the monastery controlled all this area from the minster church at Cookham. This type of early religious foundation was known as a 'double house', for both monks and nuns, and was always ruled over by an abbess. The whole complex would have consisted of a church, various communal buildings, dormitories and a guest house and was probably linked with a monastic farm.

The present church has Saxon work in the chancel which is likely to date from the time of the building of the monastery. This complex would attract an attendant settlement which is likely to have sprung up around the monastic buildings, replacing the older village at Coxborough. This new settlement on the river bank, however, would not have gone unnoticed by the Vikings when they sailed up the Thames and eventually took Reading in AD 870. The monastery was undoubtedly ransacked, and later destroyed, while the church was built again at a later date.

Soon after the birth of Alfred in AD 849, Berkshire became a county in its own right. By AD 886, Sashes Island had once more come into prominence as the site of the Saxon fort of Sceaftesege, built to defend the northern frontier of Wessex. The name Sceaftesege has developed to the modern name of Sashes via a series of medieval variations, including Shaftseies, which appears on a brass in the church dating to

1577. It is not known at what date the fort fell into disuse, but its existence would have ensured further development of the Saxon town, centred around the area of the church. In medieval times the paddock, adjacent to Cookham churchyard, was called Little Berry, a name derived from burh or bury, which in Anglo-Saxon describes a defended settlement.

In the year AD 975 Cookham came under royal ownership when the alderman, Aelpheah gave his lands at Cookham to King Edgar. Further evidence of its royal importance is given in a charter of AD 996 which records a meeting of the Witan, or Saxon government, in the village. The King's Council comprised one archbishop, three bishops, two aldermen and three abbots, as well as tenants-in-chief from all over England. Ethelred the Unready himself presided over the meeting, which has led to speculation that there may have been a royal palace in Cookham at this time.

There were further Viking raids during the years 1006–13, after which the church was rebuilt in stone, indicating a more stable period. The next mention of the settlement comes with the *Domesday Book* of 1086, which tells us that Cookham was a royal manor assessed in size as 2,400 acres with a population of 220. By this date the village had spread as far as over the moor, where a new market had been established. Additional areas of woodland belonging to the manor of Cookham were situated at Binfield and Sunninghill. Cookham Church was held by Reinbald the Priest,who also had 180 acres of land on the edge of Cookham Dean near Cannon Court and two clerics to help him administrate it. There were two mills and two fisheries on the River Thames.

In 1117 the building of an Abbey of Augustinian Canons was commenced at Cirencester and in 1133 Henry I endowed the church with 'all the state of Reinbald in lands and churches including the church at Cocheham, with lands, chapels, tithes and all other things appertaining to the said church'. This began a long association between Cookham and the Abbey of Cirencester which continued until the Dissolution in 1535. The famous Tarry Stone in the village is said to mark the boundary of the lands of the abbot.

After it became a borough in 1225 it was part of the dowry of the Queens of England until 1547. The church, meanwhile, developed in stages until 1500 when the outer building was completed as we see it today. Before the incorporation in 1582, Maidenhead was part of the royal manors of Cookham and Bray and justice was administered by the lords of the manor. The manor courts were presided over by the steward and his deputy who acted in the interests of the lord and ensured that his rights were in no way infringed. The other officers of the court included the collector, reeve, warrener, woodward, hayward, bedell, constable, tithingman and aletaster. This last job was unpaid, but as he spent his time drinking ale, there was never a shortage of volunteers for the post.

The manor court of Bray was situated in Hibbert Road, Braywick, and is described in an old deed as 'all that messuage or tenement called the Court House, lying and being within the parish of Bray, containing two rooms with a parcel of land thereunto adjoining containing by estimation one acre and a half'. The foundation date is not known but, on 6 April 1399 it was reported that the building had fallen into decay.

The Tarry Stone, a medieval boundary marker, at Cookham.

However, it was still in use in 1454 when 'the tithingman of Bray presented that the fences around the Court House were broken and out of repair'. At a later date the building was used by Hibbert Road School and then by Winbury School.

The history of the manor courts of Cookham is more confusing. The manor encompassed quite a large area including a portion of what is now Maidenhead Borough. Early reports suggested that there were two courthouses, only one of them being in the village of Cookham. The earliest was the court of 'Le Legh', which is believed to have stood close to the Maltings and Moor Hall. The first mention of this was made in 1341 on a memo of expense of the court house of Cookham made by John Laurence, the collector. He paid for 'three cartloads of straw for thatching the said house and for two cartloads of timber for the same. And for thatching and wainage. And for nails etc. to repair the walls. And for carpentry in gross'. From this description we can deduce that Le Legh was a thatched timber building which probably needed frequent repair. Further mention of the building is made in 1359 when courts were held in June and September and again in 1371 when the King's Court was held before John Weekes, the steward. In 1410, the steward James Lynde presided and in 1559, the courthouse is reported as 'fallen into decay'. No further mention is made and therefore it must be presumed that the building was not used after this date.

Perhaps the most intriguing of the court houses is the building that replaced Le Legh and the one after which Courthouse Road is named. This is first mentioned as existing in the 1582 Charter when it is a turning point in the boundary of the Borough of Maidenhead and is phrased 'from Boyn Hill as far as the Court House in the parish of Cookham and from the Court House as far as North Town'. The second mention is in 1609 when a survey records that Lord Norreys held land in Maidenhead Field next to the court house and that John Poole owned ten acres of arable land called Courthouse Close which abutted onto Brick Kiln Lane (now Courthouse Road) and the Henley Way (now St Marks Road). In 1625 it is recorded that 'money was expended in repairs of the Courthouse in Cookham'.

More definite information is given in a lease of 1771 which contains the clause 'all that old decayed house with the grounds and appurtenances situate on a green called Court House Green within the said manor (Cookham) containing three small rooms which said house was formerly used for the Courts Leet and the Courts Baron of the said Manor'. By this date the building had gone out of use and was probably superseded by accommodation in the Guildhall, erected in 1777. The building must have been timber-framed or at least in 1650 when eighteen loads of timber were stacked on Cookham Moor for use in repairing the same.

Traditionally this building is thought to have stood on a triangle of green situated at the junction of Courthouse Road and Allenby Road and opposite Boyn Grove. Until recently there was a marker board to this effect on the site. But was this the true location of the building? Rocques map of 1761, a time when the court house was supposedly still standing, shows only one building in the vicinity, situated more or less on the site of Boyn Grove. We know that Boyn Grove House was not erected until after 1857, so it is not inconceivable that the building shown is that of the old court house.

In the park behind Boyn Grove there is a raised platform measuring 100ft by 40ft which is adjacent to Muddy Lane, an ancient hollow way. Where the bank of the lane has eroded in recent years a flint foundation can be seen at the end of this platform. Is this the site of the old Cookham court house which disappeared in the late eighteenth century, but is shown on Rocques map? Excavation in the future might prove this point.

One of the most unusual inquests to be held in this court was that of John Sawyer, who, in 1680, was killed by lightning, together with his father and four horses whilst ploughing in Ham Field, Cookham. The facts were so unbelievable that an official printed document was issued relating the whole gory story and telling how the folks of Cookham 'flocked to see this as a spectacle of amazement'.

Grazebrook's Folly was perhaps better known as Strande Castle and stood on Strande Water, halfway between Maidenhead and Cookham. It was another castellated building and was erected between 1870 and 1885 by a Mr Grazebrook, an architect who was, by all accounts, an eccentric. The villagers of Cookham certainly thought so and told tales of how he patrolled the battlements with his shotgun and blasted away at imaginary raiders.

The castle had its resident ghost, a 'Grey Lady' who was said to have crossed Strande Water and entered the building each night. Although there is little foundation for this apparition, legend has it that a tower stood there in the twelfth century and leases in the record office show that Strande Water is very ancient and that there was a fishery there in medieval times.

In 1888, Mr Grazebrook erected dams at the castle to hold back the water and this brought complaints from the villagers who stated that the water at Widbrook was far too low for their cattle. Mr Grazebrook refused to remove the dams and this resulted in the incident known as 'the Battle of the Strande'. On Whit Monday, 1888, 500 men from Cookham and elsewhere stormed the castle and began removing the dam.

While Grazebrook's labourers tried to repair it they were pelted with mud by 'Peggy', a Cookham man with a wooden leg. A full scale mud-slinging session ensued which ceased when the mob captured Mr Grazebrook's hat and tore it to shreds as a token gesture. He was awarded damages in the High Court of October 1890.

Between 1900 and 1917 the castle was owned by Francis Lambert. The family of Don Ricardo lived there in the 1920s and Julius Grosscurth during the 1930s. Miss Grosscurth was the last tenant and stayed in the building until 1959, after which date deterioration took place leading to the demolition of the building in May 1968. The Grey Lady may, of course, still be resident.

The Forge in Dean Lane, Cookham Dean, dates back to the middle of the sixteenth century and is recorded by Darby as being the home of Richard Warner in 1558. Directories show that Thomas Pearce was probably the smith in 1842. Harry Hunt was in possession in 1890, followed by James Howard before it came into the hands of the present family, when Harry Crockford bought the property. After Mr Crockford's death, the forge was closed until his grandson David Matthews reopened it in 1964. Mr Matthews is still making shoes at Cookham Dean, but as his forge covered such a wide area, he has to travel in his van to fit the shoes.

The forge in Cookham High Street is perhaps one of the oldest in the area and may go back to the fifteenth century. It had a long and chequered history up to 1917 when Thomas Emmett moved to Cookham from Maidenhead and eventually took over. He remained as farrier until his death in 1949. The building is now used as a store.

Mrs Kathleen Emmett, the daughter of Thomas, lived close to the forge and gave this vivid description of its later history as she remembers it:

> It is recorded that the present dwelling house at the forge at Cookham was built in 1617 for Mr Noah Barnard, but it is probable that a shoeing forge was on this site long before this time. It would have been on the route of a horseman crossing the river at My Lady Ferry and travelling west on to Cookham Dean towards the Bath Road across Maidenhead Thicket.

When the smithy finally closed in 1949, the village no longer saw the sparks fly in the dark of a winter afternoon as the forge fire glowed red in the shadows, and the iron the smith drew from its centre was shaped by blows of the hammer, followed by lighter echoing blows on the anvil. The sight and sounds of the forge were then as familiar to the villagers as the ringing of the church bells.

After the end of the First World War and through the 1920s, Cookham was a rural place and the chief work done in smithy was farriery. However a smith was expected to be able to turn his hand to any iron work; from soldering a boy's hoop to repairing farm machinery, making candleholders for the church pews, or the lanterns provided by the parish council when the first street lights appeared in the village.

Many shire horses were used by local farmers to plough and draw farm wagons and hay carts and to perform many tasks now dealt with by mechanical means. The ploughman or carter who brought his team to the forge to be shod would ride one horse, sitting sideways on a sack thrown across its broad back, and lead the other by the bridle as they plodded steadily and obediently along the road at their usual pace. Carriage-horses, harnessed to smartly-varnished station wagons or dogcarts, would be driven to the smithy by coachmen or groom, and workhorses would be taken from the shafts of tradesmen's delivery vans and wagons. There were sturdy little cobs and ponies who drew governess carts and traps and a few riding horses and children's ponies. All came in their turn to stand patiently in the shoeing shop, fastened by their bridles to large iron rings in the wall, while their shoes were made and fitted. High on the white-washed brick wall were many iron spikes on which hung sets of four shoes, placed there by means of a long wooden pole with an inverted hook at the end. These were made for specific customers in slack hours and were reheated, fitted and nailed with some saving of time.

The day's work started early in the 1920s and '30s. Soon after seven o'clock the apprentice would arrive by bicycle. Fetching the large iron key from where it hung near the kitchen door, he unlocked the smithy and let down the heavy hinged oak shutters which fitted into the window frame. In the shoeing shop he opened the wide door, divided horizontally like a stable door, and swept the uneven ancient wooden floor. He rekindled the fire, fetched the day's supply of smith's coal and refilled the water trough. By 7.30 a.m. work had begun.

Clearly, in the early decades of the twentieth century, trade in the forge flourished. Two farriers could work side by side as the smithy contained two fires and two anvils. At one time there were four smiths working there; the master farrier, two farriers and an apprentice. However, a change came gradually over the area. With the general increase in newer farming methods, horse-power was no longer so important and the tradesmen were beginning to use motor vehicles. There were a few private motor cars, but year by year the number of horses diminished and it was necessary for smiths to look elsewhere for trade.

The day of the old-time blacksmith is over and few now remain to carry on this profession. Judging by the number of Smiths in the telephone directory, it is likely that many of them had ancestors who were in the trade.

The site of the Arbour (Hitachi Europe Ltd) is in Lower Cookham Road, Maidenhead, at the northern extent of the borough. Until around 1890 the address would have been Lower Maidenhead Road, Cookham, as this parish extended as far as Boulter's Lock. Whitebrook Park is situated on a slight rise on the Thames flood plain, which prevents the site from flooding even though the surrounding land can be underwater.

Until the 1880s the site was virgin land. It was probably best described as water meadows used for the seasonal grazing of animals. The land flooded according to the level of the water in the Thames, which would appear to have been high since the first century AD as the Romans avoided building anywhere on the flood plain. There is some evidence however, to indicate that between 3000–2000 BC the river level was low and Bronze Age people erected their flimsy farmsteads close to the Thames, which at the time was regarded as an important means of communication. Cropmarks showing enclosures and hut circles have been plotted from aerial photographs taken at the time of drought, and whilst these have not been excavated, the extent of the features are known from other sites in the Thames Valley.

By the ninth century, it would appear that the river level was high and settlements were built on the edge of the flood plain.

The land on which Whitebrook Park now stands was meadowland belonging to the Crown and this is substantiated by the entry in the *Domesday Book*. It can be seen that Reinbald the Priest, the King's chancellor, held the church and certain rectorial rights on lands within the manor, including rights to graze his animals on Widbrook Common.

By 1225, when Cookham was turned into a royal borough, the area outside the town had been subdivided into smaller manors and Whitebrook Park was land belonging to the manor of White Place or Bullocks, with the manor house situated on the north side of Widbrook Common.

Coxburrow is the earliest Saxon town of Cookham, whilst Cannon Court and Canon Hill are the strongholds of Reinbald. Elentone is the Domesday site of Maidenhead, with the present thirteenth-century town to the south.

It was during the Anglo-Saxon period that most of the Cookham fields were given names. Whitebrook Park was situated in the field known as Lower Southey. This together with Upper Southey (on higher land) made up the island of Southey. The name is derived from the Anglo-Saxon wordes 'Sutt' meaning south and 'ey', an abbreviation of 'eyot' meaning island. The whole was thus South Island. Lying south of Cookham village, this piece of land was bordered by the Thames and the Whitebrook and a ditch joining the two waterways, forming a true island.

It would appear that Lower Southey Field was an area of sixty-nine acres, as shown in three surveys. The earliest recorded ownership of the field plots occurs in the Extent of Cookham Manor in 1609 when it was divided into five plots owned by Smith, Aldridge, Austen, Prymer and Turner. Terry's survey of 1840 is more fruitful. Lower Southey is subdivided into the four main plots of Sydenham Mead Furlong, Lock Mead Furlong, Middle Shot and Cross Shot, which in turn are split up into forty-five strips of land, owned by Leycester, Fullers Brewery, Lewis, Langton, Westbrook, Skinner, Stephens, Harman and Aldridge, the last name occurring in 1609.

In the Enclosure Award of 1845, Lower Southey was made into five horizontal plots and extended into the area bordering the Whitebrook, known as Watery Butts. The plot on which the arbour was situated was owned by the trustees of the deceased

Vincent Vaughan. The other plots belonged to G.H. Leycester of White Place Farm, Thomas Lewis, the University of Oxford and William Stephens. By 1880 the majority of the land in Lower Southey Field was owned by Sir Charles Gervaise Boxall.

It was the popularity of Maidenhead as a riverside resort that encouraged building on the flood plain during the 1880s. This was not a particularly wise move, as many have found to their cost over the years. Between 1900 and 1947, floods were almost an annual occurrence, until a flood relief ditch was constructed. Since then most floods have been of a minor nature, with the exception of the recent deluge in 1990. It was around 1887 that Lower Southey Field was purchased for development by Edward Wagg. In fact. he obtained the land in nine parcels, eight of these being the property of Sir Charles Gervaise Boxall. Parcel number six was sold to Edward Wagg by George Hanbury between 1898 and 1909. George Hanbury had obtained it from Sir C.G. Boxall in 1885.

Edward Wagg started construction of Islet Park in 1891. It was a very large estate stretching from the Lower Cookham Road over to the Thames and the confluence of the White Brook. The main house, the Islet, complete with a boathouse on the White Brook, was completed in 1895. To a certain extent he was self-sufficient, with a dairy (Pine Lodge), a home farm, also known as the Bull Pen, and a herd of cows. There were acres of gardens and areas of woodland on the estate. Entry could be made either via the West Lodge on Lower Cookham Road or the South Lodge in Islet Road. The cedar walk, still in existence, was known as the Avenue and ran into the estate from the West Lodge. The road linking the South Lodge with the mansion was called the Drive. The Avenue was later than the Drive and was constructed in 1898.

Islet Park House.

The stable and water tower were built in 1903, according to the date on the metal drainpipes. Undoubtedly the stable also accommodated carriages, as in 1912 the coachman, Albert Daubeney, lived in West Lodge whilst the gardener, Daniel Philips, was residing at the South Lodge. By 1936 the stable was called the Islet Garage.

Edward Wagg, known to his family as the 'Laird', was the younger of two brothers, both senior partners in the city firm of Helbert, Wagg & Coy. He and his brother Arthur sat side-by-side in their office in Threadneedle Street. Edward was described as a white-haired gentleman with a slight stoop and short legs, who was interested in history, biography and memoirs. He was a very wealthy man and a bachelor who also owned the shooting lodge of Glenlochay in Perthshire, Scotland.

Evidence of his wealth is reflected in a dispute he had with the Hon. Waldorf Astor, an American senator, who had purchased the estate of Cliveden on the opposite bank of the Thames. Mr Astor was irritated by the gabled roof of the Islet which he maintained was spoiling his view and sent a note to Mr Wagg which read, 'The Hon. Waldorf Astor wishes to know whether Mr Wagg will sell his cottage', to which the reply read, 'Mr Wagg wishes to know whether the Hon. Waldorf Astor will sell his palace'. Edward Wagg never married but had a very good Etonian friend whom he invited for a weekend visit and who stayed for fifty-five years.

Sir Charles Boxall owned the neighbouring estate of Battlemead and on his death it passed to William Percival Gratwicke Boxall, who on 9 June 1920 sold it to the Duchy of Manchester, of which the Most Noble Angus Drages, the ninth Duke of Manchester, was the tenant for life. On the death of the duke in 1933 the property passed to the tenth duke, who sold it to the Investment & Property Trust Ltd in 1947. The house seems to have been demolished by 1935. Edward Wagg still owned the Islet estate in 1930, but shortly after this he died. The whole complex was purchased by Lady Burton, believed to be connected with the tailors of that name, by 1935. Her chauffeur, William Wills, was living in the stable building, which was then called Islet Garage. The housekeeper, Mrs Barry, occupied South Lodge, with George Shelton in 'New' Lodge, perhaps the Qudos building. William George Salmon, the head gardener, resided at Islet Gardens, which was either a new building or an old one renamed.

By 1939 Islet Park had been divided into two sections. The area near the river, surrounding the mansion, remained residential, whilst the portion off Lower Cookham Road became industrial. About 1947 C.S. Whitworth purchased the mansion and turned it into the Islet Park Hotel and Country Club.

In 1939 Courtaulds Ltd had opened a laboratory in the stable building off Lower Cookham Road. The firm had started in the twentieth century as a family silk business and was made into a public company in 1904. In 1906 they developed the process for the manufacture of rayon from viscose.

During the Second World War they remained in the stable block, but afterwards built a brand new research laboratory on the site of the arbour which was opened on 3 December 1945. By 1955 they were employing eighty-five people at Maidenhead, fifty of whom were research staff. Whilst at Maidenhead they developed the first synthetic wool, Courtelle, which was produced at their factories at Coventry and Grimsby. Maidenhead was the smallest of their six laboratories.

The artist Stanley Spencer at Cookham.

Courtaulds vacated their laboratories in 1962 and Thomas De La Rue Ltd moved into the buildings on 1 October 1962. They were trading at this time under the name Formica Ltd, having made a killing on the market with their laminated plastics. At first they too used the building for research, with twelve scientists increasing to 100 employees in the first year. On 28 December 1963, they opened a £150,000 extension to the building. De La Rue's other business was security printing and at Maidenhead they printed bank notes and stamps. On 5 March 1965, Her Majesty Queen Elizabeth II visited the site to see her face on the notes and stamps. This was the third visit to the company by a royal, the others being George V, as Duke of York in 1894, and King George VI in 1941. The Queen was greeted by the chairman, Mr A.G. Norman, and Maurice Hayes, the Mayor of Maidenhead. After visiting the research centre she inspected a seven-ton armoured vehicle designed for carrying bank notes and coins. After seeing an exhibition of stamps printed through five reigns since 1855, she was presented with a copy of the New Testament printed in gold by De La Rue in 1829. De La Rue are now operating on another part of the Islet estate.

After the Islet Park Hotel closed, the mansion was turned into flats, as it is today. For some years after the war the residential area of Islet Park was purchased by a number of owners. The next major stage of development came in 1961, when Landstone

Investments Ltd bought up the land with the intention of inserting new roads and houses. Deeds of Release of the land for development were executed on 10 July 1961. Landstone Investments had acquired most of the Islet area from Mrs Mabel Whitworth and now acquired the Battlemead portion, which they purchased from Kenneth Vasey, Kenhelm Neave and Cecile Page in three separate parcels. Having secured this land it was developed with three new roads – Battlemead Close, Islet Park and Islet Park Drive.

The Maidenhead and District Plan of May 1984 designated the industrial park a site for hi-tech industry. The old Courtaulds building was demolished and De La Rue moved into new premises nearer the river. What had been 66-68 Lower Cookham Road was developed into Whitebrook Park. Chesterfield Properties Plc and Capital & City Holdings Ltd erected The Arbour, a 93,000 sq. ft building during 1989. This office block was designed on the lines of a classical mansion, with two symmetrical wings flanking a landscaped courtyard. The old stable block (5,910 sq. ft) and the West Lodge (875 sq. ft) were included in this development.

Hitachi Europe Ltd acquired this property early in 1990 and moved in at the beginning of July. The building is now their European headquarters and houses the marketing, administration and technical development departments. The Mayor of the Royal Borough welcomed the firm to the area in June 1990 and received a cheque of £1,000 towards his benevolent fund.

Chapter Three

Bray

The parish of Bray covers a wide area which, apart from the Oakleys, includes the villages of Braywick, Holyport, Moneyrow Green and Fifield, as well as part of south Maidenhead. It is a very ancient settlement which has been part of the royal estate since the tenth century.

Bray can also be considered as one large archaeological site in so much that finds from all periods of British history have been made in the parish. Hand axes from the Old Stone Age have been found in the Thames gravels, whilst 10,000 flint implements of the Middle Stone Age were excavated by the Shaffelmoor Stream at Moor Farm, Holyport, from a Maglemosian culture dating to 8000 BC. On the opposite side of Braywick Roundabout, the New Stone Age is represented by a series of shafts which yielded pottery dated by Carbon-14 to 3320 BC, perhaps the earliest pottery ever found in Britain. Near Builders Well, bronze implements dug from the gravel are indicative of Bronze Age habitation in about 1800 BC, and a concentration of Iron Age pottery found on a riverbank site at Water Oakley represents a pre-Roman occupation. The Roman cemetery at Down Place, together with many other finds of this period, show activity in the first five centuries AD. At Moor Farm, Holyport, Saxon houses with upright wooden posts and brushwood floors have been excavated, with a radiocarbon date from the wood of AD 753.

Bray appears prominently as an entry in the *Domesday Book* of 1086 when the settlement was listed as land of the King. A church was mentioned at this time, which predates the present Church of St Michael by 300 years. The population then was around 260 persons, including three knights who undoubtedly lived in manor houses at Holyport, close to Windsor Castle. Reinbald was rector to the church and held the land at Canon Hill, Braywick.

Perhaps Bray is best known for its notorious vicar, Simon Aleyn, who died in 1565. He was the vicar of Bray featured in the poem of that name, who changed his allegiance and political view according to which sovereign was on the throne.

Was Bray a Roman settlement? Yes, if one is to believe the writing of Charles Julius Bertram, the son of a London silk dyer. In 1758 he wrote and published a book in Copenhagen which he called *Ce Situ Britanniae*, which purported to be the chronicle

Moor Farm barn during excavation.

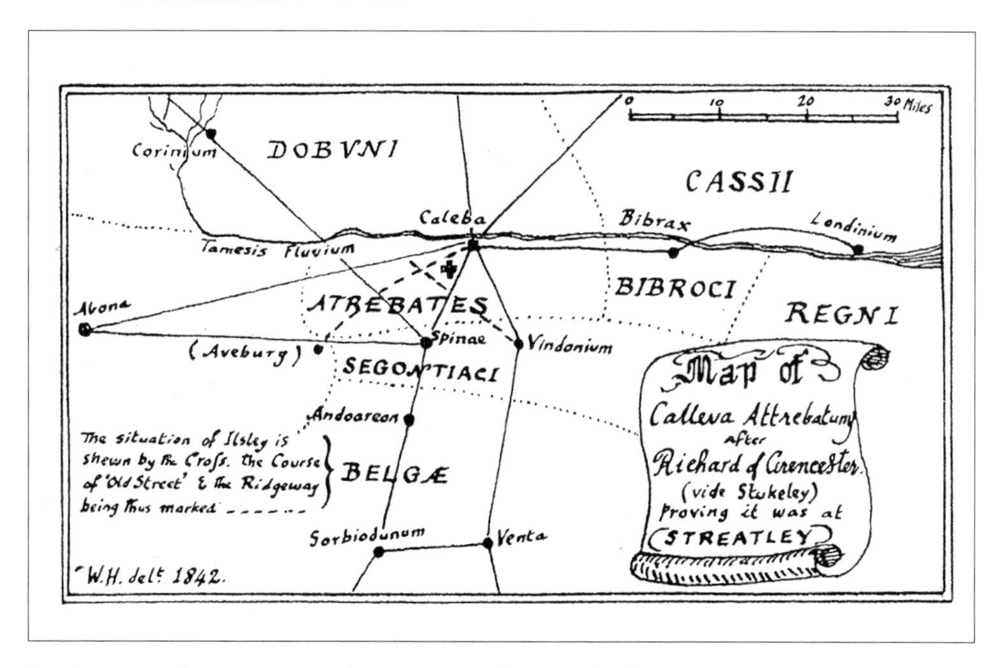

Spurious map showing Bray as the Roman settlement of 'Bibrax'.

of Richard of Cirencester, a monk of Westminster living in the fourteenth century. The book, heralded as an important historical record at the time of publication, was proved later to be a very skilful forgery, and the information it contained was about as genuine as the Piltdown Man. A large portion of Bertram's work was pure fantasy, but this was interspersed with facts taken from the Antonine Itinerary and earlier writers such as Camden, Baxter and Horsley. The fact that the book contained some element of truth misled early antiquaries like Stukeley and Colt Hoare into believing that its message was genuine, and they repeated the facts in their own writings. The Antonine Itinerary is a Roman document listing the roads and principal towns throughout the Roman Empire. The British section of this document shows that a road linking London (Londinium) with Silchester (Calleva Atrebatum) passed through the intermediate settlement of Pontibus, which was situated at the point where the road crossed the Thames. The name Pontibus, meaning 'at the bridges', has been identified as Staines, and it is only in recent years that evidence of the settlement has come to light, when foundations for high-rise buildings were being laid in the town centre. The Roman road passing through Staines, however, known locally as the Devils Highway, can be clearly traced, especially in the Easthampstead area where long sections can be seen.

When compiling his forgery Bertram decided, perhaps for mischievous reasons, to delete Pontibus from the itinerary and substitute the town Bibracte (or Bibrax). In the map reproduced here, which was drawn by Bertram and printed by Stukeley in good faith, Calleva is shown as being situated at Streatley, and Bibrax at a point where the road crosses the Thames.

Lyson, writing in 1906, reports that antiquaries were wrangling over the site of Bibracte, but had come to the conclusion that it must be Bray, Berkshire, as the Bibracte in the north of France was also known as Bray. He stated that Bray has as fair a claim as any other place in its neighbourhood to the honour of having been the Roman station of Bibracte. Bertram went further, in so much as he suggested in his map that Bibracte was the *civitas* capital of the Bibroci tribe. This rather obscure group of people was mentioned by Julius Caesar in his report on the conquest of Gaul as having been one of three tribes, the others being the Segontiaci and the Cassi, who surrendered to him just prior to his defeat of Cassivellaunus at Wheathampstead in 54 BC.

It was 100 years before Bertram's book was proved to be a forgery, and during this period many writers mentioned Bray as a Roman station on the road from London to Bath. Some gave the Roman name as Bibracte and some as Bibrax, but nobody to date seems to have appreciated that although the names are similar, they are in fact two separate towns in Roman Gaul. Bibracte was the chief town of the Aeduji, situated twelve miles west of Autun, while Bibrax was a town of the Remi tribe, a little north of the River Aisne, between Laon and Rheims. They both fell to Julius Caesar in 57 BC.

Despite the final realisation that the river crossing at Bibracte was pure invention on the part of Bertram, and that the road crossed at a point some twelve miles distant at Staines, one might still today ask the question, 'Was Bray a Roman settlement?' Charles Kerry, in 1851, wrote of numerous Roman antiquities and coins of nine emperors being found at Down Place, and human remains and foundations being discovered in the gardens to the west of the house. He publishes a long list of coins found in the area from Bray churchyard to the river. Kerry also gives details of the so-called Alderman Silver's Roman Road, which has been traced from Braywick to Cockmarsh and passes through the centre of the town. Sections of the road can be detected at Braywick Cemetery, Stafferton Lodge and in Kidwells Park, the last-named section being examined when the relief road was built without producing any conclusive dating evidence.

The Bray Court Rolls of 1336 mention one field near the river which was named 'Ere-Burgh-Feld Apud Ocle' and could be interpreted as meaning 'the field of the former town.' In 1970, in an area adjacent to this field, Christopher Stanley with the Middle Thames Archaeological Society excavated a Roman site of considerable proportions. The site turned out to be a burial ground with a large number of inhumations and some cremated remains stored in pottery vessels. Most of the skeletons uncovered showed signs of deformities, with missing limbs and crippling arthritis in the bones. Some of the skulls had holes bored in the top, an ancient and usually fatal method of releasing pressure on the brain. It was considered that this might be the site of a primitive Roman hospital, as amputations and other mutilations had taken place. Examination of the skeletons showed that nearly all the persons died at a very early age. Grave goods, indicating that the burials must have been pagan, date the interments to between AD 320 and AD 400. Nearby, wooden posts were located on the riverbank, which may have been a landing stage or flimsy bridge.

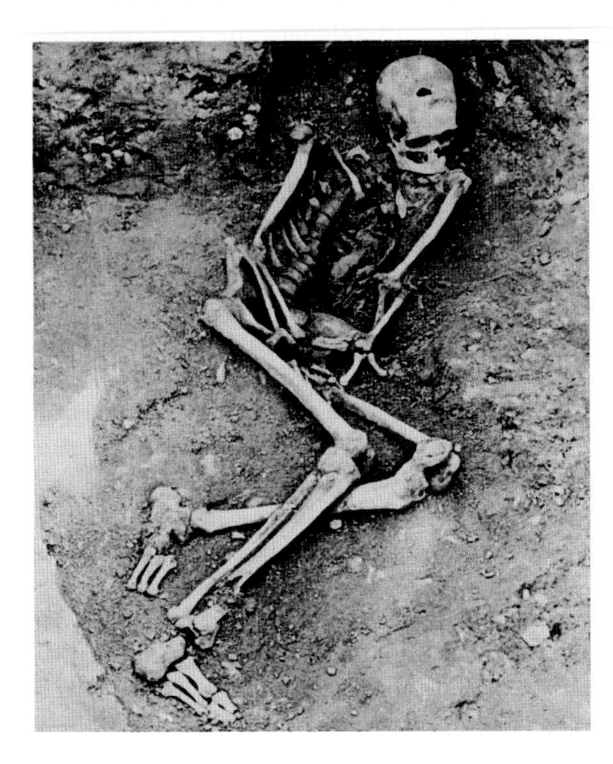

A skeleton from the Roman cemetery at Bray.

Two years later, in the grounds of Down Place Cottage, some two-dozen skeletons were uncovered by floodlight in advance of a destructive bulldozer, and were assumed to be part of the same burial ground, making the whole cemetery at least a quarter of a mile in diameter. Could this glut of burials then be considered evidence of an extensive Roman settlement in the vicinity? Perhaps, ironically, Bertram's invention may prove nearer the truth than he ever imagined.

An archaeological evaluation carried out in 1991 by R.P. S. Clouston on a site of a proposed golf course at Cruchfield Manor, Bray, has produced evidence of a village which disappeared sometime during the medieval period. With the exception of the present manor house and farm, which are of later date, no sign of this settlement can be seen above ground.

The site has been designated as a Deserted Medieval Village (DMV) and such settlements were normally wiped out by the Black Death in the fourteenth century; by early monks who required solitude, or by some form of enclosure of land. The only other example of a DMV in the area is Shottesbrooke, where the Norman village of the goldsmiths and charcoal burners was erased by emparkment in the seventeenth century. The earliest mention of the manor of Cruchfield, or Lords Lands as it was also known, was in 1185 when it was recorded as 'Kerchesfield'. The name is thought to mean the 'field of the cross', probably because it lies on the boundary of Bray and Warfield.

A perambulation of Bray parish in 1272 indicates that a cross was made on an old oak tree to delineate the parish boundary. The other name, Lords Lands, probably derives from the fact that it was originally a royal dairy, belonging to the King at Windsor. Like all other 'field' names in the area (Warfield, Winkfield, Binfield) it was originally a clearing in the Royal Forest of Windsor, and therefore much under the eye of the monarch. Documentary evidence suggests that the demise of the village may have been due to its enclosure for the purpose of providing pasture or additional arable land. This may have been as late as 1450.

The manor of Cruchfield, formed by subinfeudation in the twelfth century, was held by Geoffrey de Baggsite in 1186 and passed to Henry Lovell in 1250. Eventually, under the title of Lords Lands, it was bequeathed to the Fishmongers Company in 1609 to help support Jesus Hospital in Bray.

The question now arises as to whether the deserted village equates with the lost Domesday site of 'Bras', which was situated in the ancient hundred of Bray. In the *Domesday Book* this lost manor was mentioned as being one hide, or 120 acres, in size – the same acreage as Cruchfield was when held by Henry Lovell in 1272. Before the Norman Conquest in 1066 it was held by the Saxon lord Ted, from Edward the Confessor, after which it passed to Alwin, son of Chipping, who held it from William I. It is described as having enough arable land for one plough and a population of around forty people. Perhaps the most interesting fact was that it had its own church, separate from the mother church at Bray. This is the only medieval church in East Berkshire of which, at present, we have no account. Evidence of early settlement at Cruchfield shows up on an aerial photograph taken in 1980 where chalk, probably used as an early building material, is seen to be ploughed up near the surface. Closer scrutiny also shows the shape of possible buildings on the site.

Bray Church and Chantry.

In June 1996 the Maidenhead 700 Pageant celebrated the year 1296, when the town officially took on the earlier name of Maidenhythe from the New Wharf which had been put up by Maidenhead Bridge. Prior to this date, the settlement on the borders of Cookham and Bray had been known as South Ellington.

In 1296 Edward I was on the throne but there was no Queen of England. Edward's mother, Queen Eleanor, had died in 1291 while his first wife, also named Eleanor, passed away in 1290. And Edward's second wife was Queen Marguerite, whom he did not marry until 1299. The fact that England was without a Queen for eight years from 1291 to 1299 presents a local puzzle.

The Bray Court Rolls record that in the year 1293 Bray Church was built, with the Queen as patron, and moreover that she was having difficulty in extracting money from her tenants and parishioners to pay for construction. She apparently commanded the beadle of the manor, a parish official, together with the church wardens to raise the said assessment from those who refused to pay it. This poses the fascinating question as to who the person actually responsible for the construction of the church was? Queen Eleanor was dead and Queen Marguerite had not even formed an alliance with Edward in 1293. Bray was also part of the Queen's dowry, but with no Queen on the horizon, who gave the orders to the beadle? This Queen-less environment is emphasised in another deed dated 12 June 1293 when the King himself ordered the Keeper of Windsor Forest to cause Ralph de lvyngho to have in that forest six oaks fit for timber to make a house thereof for the use of the chaplain celebrating in the King's chapel for the souls of King Henry III and Queen Eleanor, the King's parents, and his late wife, Queen Eleanor.

This deed has hitherto been attributed to the chapel of St Andrew and Mary Magdalene at Maidenhead. But it is unlikely to have been so because worship in that chapel was prohibited by the Bishop of Salisbury between 1270 and 1324, and therefore there was no chaplain.

The King's chapel referred to in the deed is more likely to have been the small chantry of the Blessed Virgin Mary at Bray, erected in the first place to pray for the souls of those already mentioned. This was standing in 1293 and had a chaplain at the time, recorded as Thomas atte Grenedowne. Queen Marguerite did however make a royal grant of land in Bray to Adam le Spicer in 1313. This land was used for the construction of Copped Hall, close by the old Market Hall in Maidenhead. This building was demolished in 1751, prior to the building of the Guildhall in the centre of the town in 1777.

In modern society, mistresses and any resulting illegitimacy tend to evoke little comment. In past centuries, however, such goings on were frowned upon, and if the liaison involved a royal personage or someone in the public eye, then details of their bedroom habits would be hastily swept under the carpet, or at least under the bed in question.

This is the story of two such accommodating ladies and their offspring, which spans a period of 300 years. Both ladies have several things in common. Apart from being female, they were both mistresses to royalty, both actresses as well as being talented, desirable and ambitious. On top of which they both lived locally for a period of their lifetime, albeit that details of their activities here are a bit hazy. The earliest of these was Nell Gwyn, actress and mistress to Charles II. According to the Ashmole papers in a museum at Oxford, she was born on 2 February 1660. Historians in Hereford claim that she was born in a house in Pipe Well Lane, Hereford, whilst more popular accounts assign the place of her birth to Coal Yard, Drury Lane. She was born of working-class parents and was illiterate, such letters of hers that exist having been written by other people. Her mother, Eleanor, after whom she was named, died of drowning after staggering drunkenly into the river near her house at Millbank in 1679. Her father was said to be a fruiterer in Drury Lane. This last point is probably correct as Nell's first job was as an orange seller in the Theatre Royal, Drury Lane, where she sold her wares in a pit assigned to such vendors. Whilst in the theatre she had several influential lovers, who helped her to aspire from the vending pit onto the stage of the Theatre Royal. Her first performance took place in 1665 when she played Cydaria in Dryden's *Indian Emperor*. She continued as an actress until 1682, after which she quit the stage.

The story of King Charles admiring her oranges is perhaps a little far-fetched, and if the truth were known, he was probably more interested in her navel than her Navels. He first set eyes on her as she was reciting an epilogue whilst spread-eagled on a large coaching wheel. He admired her figure and invited her to travel in his coach and have supper, after which he made her his mistress. Once she was in royal favour, Nell never looked back, and her popularity increased when her Catholic rival, the Duchess of Portsmouth, started a smear campaign. When mistaken for her rival at Oxford, Nell quipped, 'Pray, good people, be civil. I am the Protestant whore'.

Her first son was born on 8 May 1670, and in the presence of the King she called him a bastard, pleading that she had no other name to call him. The King took the hint and created him Baron Heddington and Earl of Burford, and later Duke of St Albans. A second son, James, was born in 1671. Nell stayed in favour with Charles for the rest of his life and was maintained, it is reported, at vast expense. His dying request to his brother was, 'let not poor Nellie starve.'

The merry monarch paid many visits to Windsor during his reign, and to ensure that Nell was by his side, he assigned to her Burford House, close by the castle walls. In addition to this she also lived in the mansion of Philberds at Holyport, an ancient manor house which had been in existence since 1248, when it was occupied by Hugh de St Philibert. Whilst in Windsor the King often dined in the Dukes Head in Peascod Street with his wayward friend George Villiers, Duke of Buckingham, who lived in Cliveden House. Together they would ride to Holyport to visit Nell. The last house at Philberds was demolished earlier this century and only the building platform and part of the moat can now be seen in a field at the end of Holyport Street.

Many said that Nell's bust was her fortune, and she must have had this in mind when she asked Sir Peter Lely to design busts of her to stand in various properties. Such a bust existed at Philberds but was eventually transferred to Bramshill House, Hampshire. Nell Gwyn died on 16 November 1687 of an apoplexy after a short but eventful life, and was buried in St Martins in the Fields.

Nearly 200 years later, on 13 October 1853, a daughter, Emilie Charlotte Le Breton, was born to the Dean of Jersey at the rectory, St Saviour, Jersey. She was nicknamed Lillie at a very early date as her skin was so white. In 1874 she married wealthy widower Edward Langtry in Jersey and moved to London. And so Lillie Langtry entered high society.

It was Lord Ranelagh who introduced her to the fashionable crowd, and it was not long before the fresh young girl from the sticks appearance made her the toast of the town. Men were captivated by her, and notables like Oscar Wilde came to call on her. Sir John Millais painted her and was the first to call her the Jersey Lily. Whistler also captured her on canvas. Despite her husband, she took many lovers, one of whom is recorded as saying, 'Lilies can be dreadfully boring when not planted in a bed.'

But if Frewen found her boring, the Prince of Wales, and heir to the throne, did not. He first met her on 24 May 1877 at a dinner party and insisted on monopolising her for the whole evening. The Princess Alexandra was away and for the next few days he drove and rode with Lillie openly in Rotten Row. When the Princess returned she seemed to condone the Prince's infidelity and made a trio with them during the 1877 season.

Edward Langtry was none too pleased at being cuckolded, but continued to pay for Lillie's extravagances. She was eventually presented at the palace to Queen Victoria, who, well aware of her son's indulgences, stared straight ahead and assumed her 'we are not amused' look. The Prince of Wales, or Bertie as Lillie called him, was classified as a rake. Apart from his women, he liked lots of good food and enormous cigars. He enjoyed mixing with society at Maidenhead, eating at Skindles, and being entertained at parties at Taplow Court and Cliveden. He also regularly attended race meetings at Ascot where many of his own horses ran. It was probably during this period when he reputedly rented or purchased Bray Lodge in the Fisheries as a place to liaise with his mistress Lillie. It was large and well-situated with lawns running down to the river.

Lillie became pregnant with her only child, Jeanne Marie, in 1880. The father was not named but the conclusions were obvious. The following year the Prince tired of the affair and went off to pastures new. Nevertheless, he did turn up at Lillie's stage debut in *She Stoops to Conquer* at the Haymarket in December 1881.

Edward Langtry died in 1897 and in 1899 Lillie remarried to Hugo de Bathe. Just after 1900 she left the stage and retired to Monaco, where on 12 February 1929 she died. She was buried in St Saviour's churchyard, Jersey, in a grave with a marble bust of herself on a granite base, She was not a great actress, but will be remembered for her remarkable beauty and her liaison with Bertie, Prince of Wales.

Cox Green is one of those settlements whose name seems to defy interpretation and may well have to remain that way. As a normal rule, most local place names can be traced back to the Anglo-Saxon dialect and when translated, provide an adequate and explainable description of the site. But who or what was Cox? That is the question that needs to be answered if the mystery is to be solved.

Evidence seems to indicate that the name did not come into use until the late nineteenth century, and early maps show it to be an area of arable land within the manor and parish of Bray. The main development period occurred after the Second World War and since then, thousands of houses have been erected. Cox Green has become an entity in its own right, with a community centre in Highfield Lane. Not surprising perhaps as the A423 motorway spur, which began in 1939 as the Maidenhead Bypass, separated the settlement from the rest of Maidenhead, placing Cox Green fairly and squarely south of the border.

In the thirteenth century, the lands which are now Cox Green belonged to the medieval manors of Ockwells, Shoppenhangers and Lowbrooks. The former, which emerged as Ockholt in 1267 when it was held by Richard Norreys, probably originated as a hunting lodge in Windsor Forest. The present manor house was built

Shoppenhangers Manor (now demolished).

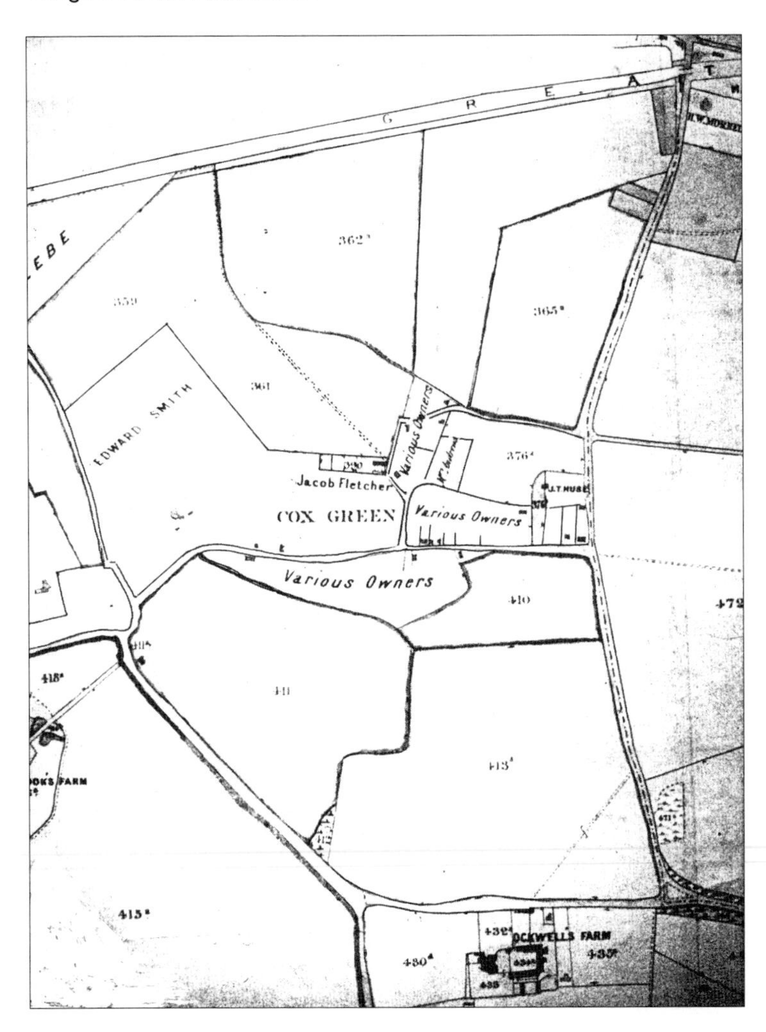

Map showing the original Cox Green, before expansion.

by Sir John Norreys about 1449 and together with stables, barns and outbuildings formed a complex grouped around a courtyard.

Roger de Shobenhangre is recorded as holding that manor as early as 1204, but the present building only dates to 1915, when it was erected by antique dealer Thornton Smith using old materials from demolished buildings. The manor of Lowbrooks, now known as Lillebrooke Manor, dates back to 1292 when Robert de Lollebrook was the owner. All three manors were later acquired by the Grenfell family, first Shoppenhangers in 1801, then Ockwells in 1813 and finally Lowbrooke in 1860. The Grenfells, later the Desboroughs, were the largest landowners around Maidenhead by 1900, and an estate map showing the extent of their lands can be seen in their former manor house, Taplow Court.

The first mention of any properties in the area of Cox Green occurs in a grant of 1621 for a charity set up by Sir John Norreys of Ockwells Manor. Houses were to be provided for all poor, aged or impotent persons of Bray parish to live in certain parcels

The manor of Moors at Holyport.

of ground, and six of the cottages were located somewhere near to the Foresters public house. The first two were in the possession of Anne Clayton (1799) and William Clayton (1817), ancestors of the well-known Cox Green family. Others belonged to Thomas Johnson (1799), Matthew Sawyer (1699) and Richard Franklyn (1699). The administrator of the charity was one Thomas Wilcox, whose name, if shortened through illiteracy from Thomas William Cox, could conceivably have given his name to the settlement.

By map evidence Cox Green, together with its name, seems to have come into being between the years 1792 and 1817. An enclosure map of 1817 specifically names the settlement and shows eighteen houses in existence situated on both sides of Cox Green Lane. In 1761 a few houses were sited between the Foresters and Lock Lane, while the area west of the Green was part of Maidenhead Thicket.

By 1770 horseracing was taking place at Boyn Hill Racecourse, which stretched from Tittle Row to Cox Green. This was in existence until 1801 and was visited by the King in 1787.

On the edge of the thicket at the west end of Cox Green Lane stood the residence of Old Court, which seems to have been of some antiquity. This large house, which was taken over by British Filters in April 1944, may have stood on the site of the court of the canons of Waltham Abbey, who held the manors of Heywood at Woodlands Park. Cannon (Canon) Lane, which was linked to Old Court by Highfield Lane, was also an old route used by the Waltham canons.

Having established that a small hamlet existed by about 1800, we can now give further consideration to the name. The Green, which is still extant – although perhaps diminished in size – would be a piece of common land where animals could graze, perhaps when being driven to market. The prefix 'Cox', bearing in mind the late development of the settlement, is most likely to be a personal name. A check through the Bray records shows that there are at least twenty-five entries of the name between the years 1662 and 1797. Sometimes the spelling is Cocks or Cochs, but it is not unusual for the letters 'ck' or 'ch' to be replaced by an 'x', being the Greek symbol for the first two letters of Christ's name, as in the shortened word 'Xmas'.

Some proof of Cox being a personal name comes from a row of old dwellings in Lock Lane, known as Cox's Cottages. This would appear to indicate that they were built by or for a person called Cox. An extensive search, however, has not revealed any landowner or noteworthy person of that name, unless it was the aforementioned Thomas Wilcox. One long shot is that there may be some connection with Richard Cox (1777-1846) who developed the Cox's Orange Pippin. This famous apple came from a strain of the Ribstone Pippin and was first recognised in 1825 at the Colnbrooke nursery of a Mr Smale. Could it be that William Cox conducted some early trials at Cox Green? There were certainly extensive market gardens and orchards where a variety of apples were grown, many of which are immortalised in the road names of the Apple estate built by Sunway Homes. A further coincidence is that the Smales family were developers in Cox Green and built some large properties in Highfield Lane.

The Brill family were farmers and fruit growers over a long period in Cox Green. They leased large areas of land and owned several houses, including Rose Cottages, which were built for their workers. They also developed the Brilson herd of Wessex Saddleback pigs which lived in the orchard paddocks and in pigsties at Common Farm, now Stratford Gardens. Wessex Way is named after these pigs, although the other roads on the council estate are called after Saxon kingdoms, towns and saints. The Brills still live at Homer Farm in Cox Green Lane.

Next to Homer Farm is Beehive Manor, which was also associated with the Brill family. One of their number is said to have been the innkeeper when this building was the Dog & Partridge. At that time, it was a two-storey building which was later converted into a farmhouse and bakery. The name comes from the beehives which were placed in the garden by a Mr Haynes, while 'manor' was added as a status symbol.

In the early twentieth century it was held by a Mrs Hyde, an antique dealer, who sold it to Mr Appleton, a millionaire, who extended the building and added a third storey. In the 1930s it was a weekend home, with many showbiz parties being held there. Appleton went broke around 1940 and moved in with his butler and cook, Mr and Mrs Lightfoot, as their lodger! During the war, the manor was let to the Duke of Manchester after a German family had been hounded out, and was then converted into six flats. Clock Cottage, on the opposite side of the road, was built in 1936 with old timbers from a house in Stoke Poges, and was briefly let to Jim Mollison, husband of Amy Mollison, the well-known pilot.

The nucleus of Cox Green was situated close to the green itself and down Lock Lane, named after Grannie Lock who lived in a thatched cottage there. The Foresters and the Barley Mow were the two local pubs. The Post Office was built in 1939 – at the time it was a distinct settlement from Maidenhead. Where Sherbourne Drive is now, there was a house owned by Mrs Fletcher and a small holding in the possession of the Vanes who owned Ellay Tubes. During the Festival of Britain in 1951, the Vanes erected a skylon similar to that on the South Bank in London.

Among those buildings that have disappeared from the landscape are Victory Hall and the Church of the Good Shepherd. The former was created after the First World War from an old Army hut and was later used as a community centre for whist drives, film shows and dances. The earliest record of the church was in 1874 when it was a Primitive Methodist chapel. It was purchased by All Saints in 1911 when an apse and porch were added, and became separated again from Boyn Hill in 1975. Both of these buildings were demolished and incorporated in the new community centre, built around 1970 from donations and the sale of the Victory Hall site.

One of the outlying residences was the Points, which was home to both Countess Annesley and Lady Fairfax. Another was Kimbers House, held by Mr and Mrs Ford, of blotting paper fame, in 1914. During the war, the grounds were used to house German and Italian prisoners of war, and later for the Cox Green Flower Show which was organised annually for thirty-seven years by the secretary, Mr Bedford. It was usually held on a Thursday and gardeners from thirty miles around came to exhibit their produce.

It was after the Second World War that Cox Green expanded in all directions. To the east, the Larchfield estate wiped out all but a fragment of Curls Lane. To the north, the Wessex estate reached Highfield Lane. And to the south, the Apple Estate and Ockwells Park covered a majority of the open ground. The ancient green was almost completely lost within the suburban sprawl.

One cannot write about Cox Green without mentioning what must have been the earliest house, now lost beneath the flats in Northumbria Road. This was the Roman villa, found and excavated in 1959, which was in use from the first to the fourth centuries AD. The villa had four stages of rebuilding and had eighteen rooms in its final stage, which included a baths suite. The finds indicated that the owner was involved in the growing of cereals; one can imagine that in Roman times Cox Green was mainly fields of golden wheat. A plaque on the block of flats now marks the spot of this building. Cox Green now has a parish and community of its own, and is no longer reliant on the facilities of Maidenhead. It may even have its own railway station at some time in the future. We may not know where Cox Green came from, but we certainly know where it is going.

All Maidonians will know a little of the chequered history of White Waltham Airfield, which has been in operation for nearly sixty years, but probably only a few know that in 1929 Maidenhead had its own aerodrome. This was situated at Bray by the junction of the Holyport and Windsor roads, on land belonging to the Good family at Stroud Farm. Although aircraft design was still in its infancy, the possibility of using places for commercial purposes on a local scale was visualised soon after the First World War. From 1919, many towns began constructing their own civil aerodromes. The major site for London had been set up at Croydon, but the lack of landing places in the provinces was holding back the establishment of an aerial network throughout the country.

The Air Ministry was encouraging local authorities to provide aerodromes, and in 1928 South Bucks and the Thames-side Regional Committee made the following statement:

> The question of making provision for the reservation of suitable sites for the purposes of future air traffic should not be overlooked and the circular letter on this subject from the Air Ministry to Local Authorities, issued in October 1928, should promote a wider interest in the possibilities of establishing municipal and private aerodromes and thus incidentally assist in the reservation of open space.

Accordingly, Maidenhead reacted to this challenge and arrangements were made for an aerodrome to be sited at Bray. The entrepreneur behind the venture was Donald Stevenson, who was an automobile and aeronautical engineer with a business in Station Approach, Maidenhead. Mr Stevenson was no stranger to aviation, and had been connected with it since the early experimental days. Since 1907 he had worked for various aircraft companies and had ended up as production engineer for Wycombe Aircraft Constructors Ltd, High Wycombe, in 1919. Since 1920 he had been an engineer for GWK Cars at Maidenhead, but he continued to patent several inventions in connection with aviation.

In May 1929 the town council approved the plan and accepted an invitation to attend the opening ceremony. It was recorded in the minutes that an enterprise of this nature was of much importance and had the support of the council. The Grand Opening Ceremony took place on 8 June 1929 at 2.30 p.m., when the Mayor of Maidenhead, Councillor W. Archer, cut the tape which was fastened to the tail of an AVRO aeroplane. Well over 1,000 people were present on the field, with large crowds on the surrounding roads who were hoping to get a glimpse of the aeronautics. Fourteen aircraft were lined up for inspection by the public, including many biplanes of the Moth type and a selection of monoplanes. Some people had never been that close to an aeroplane before and took full advantage of the opportunity.

All the magnificent men were there, together with their own personal flying machines. Not least of all was Captain G. De Havilland, who gave a display in one of the latest all-metal coupe Moths. Other air aces included Captain Broad, chief test pilot for De Havilland, and Captains Davis, Jones and Pickthorn, instructors at the Brooklands School of Flying. The aptly-named Mr Tranum demonstrated the use of the parachute, but could find no takers when he offered the public a chance to jump.

Maidenhead Aerodrome

(Entrance from Windsor Road).

Proprietors: DONALD STEVENSON & Co., Ltd.

A Grand Opening Display

OF

.FLYING.

On SATURDAY NEXT, June 8th,

AT 2 30 P.M.

HIS WORSHIP THE MAYOR (Councillor W. Archer), supported by Members of the Town Council, has kindly consented to open the Aerodrome.

EXHIBITION FLIGHTS

BY WELL-KNOWN PILOTS

who have kindly offered to assist, including :

Capt. G. de HAVILLAND, O.B.E., A.F.C.,
designer of the famous " Moth " Light Aeroplane,

Capt. H. S. BROAD, A.F.C.,
Chief Test Pilot of the de Havilland Aircraft Cc., Ltd.

Capt. H. D. DAVIS, A.F.C.
Managing Director of the Brooklands School of Flying,

Capt. E. A. JONES & Major C. M. PICKTHORN, M.C.,
Instructors of the Brooklands School of Flying.

PASSENGER FLIGHTS

By the Instructors of the

BROOKLANDS SCHOOL OF FLYING

ENTRANCE TO GROUND 6d. **Cars Parked Free.**

Refreshments by the "SPORTSMAN RESTAURANT."

Phone : Maidenhead 1111. Telegrams : " Planes, Maidenhead."

DONALD STEVENSON & Co., Ltd.,

Automobile & Aeronautical Engineers & Agents,

STATION APPROACH, MAIDENHEAD.

Advert for the opening of Maidenhead Aerodrome in 1929.

However, there was much more enthusiasm shown for the passenger flights, which were being offered at 5*s* a time. The first to accept was Alderman Cox, several times Mayor and a freeman of the borough. At the age of eighty-nine, he was determined to try out the new-fangled machine, with the comment, 'You have to do things for the time, even at my age'. He was accompanied by the Deputy Mayor of Maidenhead, Councilor Norris. After the flight the alderman said, 'I enjoyed it immensely, I shall certainly do it again.'

The opening day was a great success. But the aerodrome was to prove a four-month wonder, and by October 1929 it had been closed by a court action. Local inhabitants complained about disturbance and noise and were doubtful of the safety of the aircraft. One gentleman from Bray made these points to *The Advertiser* when he wrote:

> The charm and peace of Bray are already a thing of the past and it appears now that even the sky is defiled. We are overrun with noisy cars and noisy people as it is. Must they be in the heavens as well as on earth?

The last recorded event at the aerodrome was a visit by Sir Alan Cobham, a famous airman whose pioneer flights to India, Australia and Africa were epoch-making events in aerial navigation. Sir Alan's machine was a 500hp Armstrong-Siddeley engined giant De Havilland Moth, which seated twelve in the cabin. The object of his visit was to give rides to schoolchildren and promote 'airmindedness' among the rising generation.

For a short period, passenger flights continued at another unrecorded airfield in the vicinity. This may have been at Cockmarsh, Cookham, which is known to have been used as a landing place at some time in the past. The Windsor Road airfield was spasmodically used for private flying until the mid-1940s, although it had officially been closed as an aerodrome. It was still being used at the end of the Second World War, and at a later date for gliding purposes.

Chapter 4

Oakley – Vampires and Monkeys

The Oakleys are a group of settlements in the manor and parish of Bray, comprising Oakley Green, East Oakley and Water Oakley. The name is derived from the Old English 'acleah' which translates as a clearing in an oak wood. In the Bray context, the oak wood refers to Windsor Forest – a vast area laid out by the Norman Kings for hunting purposes. On the Norden map of 1607, the perimeter of this forest is shown to be seventy-seven miles in circumference, although 300 years earlier it had been even larger. Today the remaining portions make up Windsor Great Park. The oak was the main tree in Windsor Forest, and there are many records of trees being cut down and transported to Windsor and Maidenhead for repairs to the wooden bridges crossing the Thames. Other local place names in the area which have connections with the oak forest are Ockholt or Ockwells Manor, Bray and Oakingham, the older name for Wokingham.

Oakley Green, which is probably the oldest settlement, is likely to have evolved as an assart, or clearing, hewn out of the forest. As the village extended towards Windsor, East Oakley came into existence, and then finally Water Oakley, being that part of the settlement located along the banks of the river. The whole complex may well have been in existence in Anglo-Saxon times. Indeed, Oakley has a strong claim to being the site of Acleah, mentioned as a battlefield in the *Anglo-Saxon Chronicles* from AD 851. It is recorded that the Danes assembled at the mouth of the Thames, stormed Canterbury and London, and proceeded up the river and to the south. At this point, the chronicler tells us, King Ethelwulf and his son Ethelbald, with the West Saxon levies 'fought against them at Acleah, and there made the greatest slaughter of a heathen host that we have heard tell of up to this present day, and there won a victory'.

Obviously, we have no positive proof of this incident taking place at Bray, but there is a tradition of a battle being fought on Bray Downs, which equates to the rising ground near Oakley Court after which Down Place took its name. Also the name 'Batlyng-mede' occurs in the Bray Court Rolls in 1336, which would appear to indicate the site of some ancient skirmish. In common with most medieval settlements, the name of Oakley appears in many different forms due to widespread illiteracy amongst the early inhabitants. Examples are Aukeley (1220), Acle (1296), Okle (1373),

Ockley (1572), and later Okeley. These all occur in legal and official documents, where in each case the lawyer or clerk was uncertain of the correct spelling.

The original village of Oakley Green was located on the Saxon (and later packhorse) route linking Windsor with Reading, now represented by the B3024. The green itself was an area of common land on either side of the road where villagers grazed their animals. Kimbers Farm, located in the village, was mentioned in the year 1288 when it belonged to Walter Wodeward of Oakley. An ancient homestead moat at Mills Farm represents the old house of 'Sheeres', which is reputed to have been an inn for packhorse travellers. East Oakley, as the name suggests, is represented by the area east of Oakley Green which extends northwards to Bullocks Hatch Bridge and the Willows. In 1288, Bishops Farm is mentioned as belonging to Michael Bishop. The manor house of Bullocks, now long gone, was owned in 1292 by Robert Bullock. There was a watermill at East Oakley in 1451, when it was recorded that Robert West took excessive toll. Water Oakley is a long, narrow settlement extending from Bullocks Hatch Bridge in the west. These two points lay on the A308, which marks the boundary to the south, whilst the Thames bounds the area to the north. Water Oakley has never been a highly populated area, and undoubtedly owes its existence to the wharf which once stood on the site of the court. Being close to Windsor Forest, it was probably extensively used for the despatch of timber over many centuries, and one document of 1535 records that 'the Bishop of Winchester shipped quantities of oak to his estate at Billingbear in Windsor Forest from Water Oakley'. The Wharf, however, was in use at a much earlier period. The first reference appears to have been in 1305 when Robert Glodeman is listed as 'the collector of tolls at Ocle'. By 1333. Reginald Belen was the tithing man and toll collector, and in that year he 'paid the sum of 8*s* for sixteen boats which had passed in the course of a year'. In 1373 John Cur, a local businessman, 'gave to the lord of the manor 4*s* per annum for wharfage at Okle'.

After Down Place was built, the land on which Oakley Court now stands, together with the wharf, became part of the estate of that mansion. Sir Robert Jones bought Down Place in 1518 and the conveyance records that 'in that year Richard Weston granted to Sir Robert Jones a piece of land called Quenes-Warfe lying between Down Place on the west and his land called Bawdwyne Botelers on the east'. This probably requires some explanation.

Queens Wharf is the earlier title for Water Oakley Wharf, and probably takes its name from the same source as Queens Eyot, a small island in the Thames close to the court. The prefix 'Queens' is likely to elude to the fact that Bray was a royal manor, and that for a long period the land was always vested in the Queen consort. The reference to the land called 'Bawdwyne Botelers' is yet another example of local illiteracy. The person in question, who owned the land in 1498, was the Bray parish clerk, Baldwin Boteler. His name, in turn, probably originated from the time when names and trades were often linked, as in Baldwin the Bottler. However, what his family bottled is unknown! In 1627, John Page of Down Place owned Oakley Wharf, of which James Ewst is listed as tenant. For some time after that it was referred to as 'Page's timber wharf'. By 1800 maps show that a small community had built up around the landing place, and whilst one might be tempted to call this a village, it was probably made up of workers on the Down Place estate. However, Norden's map of 1607 clearly shows the existence of a village to the east of Oakley Court, with several houses and access to the main road. But today, apart from a small estate of houses near Bray Studios, the settlement of Water Oakley has dwindled and has now taken on the status of a postal district.

Oakley Court

Oakley Court Hotel is situated on the banks of the Thames at Water Oakley. The court was originally erected for Richard Hall-Saye JP in 1859 on land he purchased from the adjoining estate of Down Place. There is no record of the name of the architect, but he may be the same person who designed New Lodge, one mile to the south, which was completed in 1858. Mr Hall-Saye was born at Downham, Norfolk, in 1827 and assumed the surname and arms of Saye in conformity with the will of his uncle, the Reverend Henry Saye, when he died in 1855. He travelled to Bray where he met and married Ellen Evans of Boveney Court, Buckinghamshire, in August 1857. From this union came two sons and four daughters. He was appointed High Sheriff of Berkshire in 1864 and a Justice of the Peace in 1865.

Oakley Court, *c.* 1979.

Charles Kerry, an historian and schoolmaster from Bray, visited Oakley Court in 1861 and wrote:

> This Gothic mansion, the seat of Richard Hall-Saye, was erected on the ground formerly called Queens or Water Oakley Wharf, mentioned in the account of Down Place. The building is an admirable specimen of the adaption of the ancient baronial style to the requirements of the ninteenth century. The hall is spacious and contains a staircase of medieval design. The furniture throughout is oak. In a window in the library are the arms of Saye and Morley in stained glass.

Another writer described it as a:

> Victorian Neo-Gothic building with stock brickwork, regular black pointed jointing and stone quoins. Timber windows have been fitted into tone mullions. The stone fascias and friezes are extensively decorated. Gargoyles with forked tails, scaled bodies and ferocious muzzle jaws can be seen on the apex and the sides of the spires which abound. The building has steep gable roofs with a castellated tower to one side.

Mr Hall-Saye sold the estate in spring 1874 and moved to Ives Place, an old manor house which stood on the site of the present Maidenhead Town Hall. During the 'Great Fire of Maidenhead', which occurred the following year at Langton's Brewery, he proved himself a hero by saving all the horses in the brewery stables. He also organised the removal of several hundred barrels of beer which were stacked in the marketplace, much to the delight of the local inhabitants!

The new owner of Oakley Court was Lord Otto Fitzgerald, a peer of whom little seems to have been recorded. When he moved into the building in 1874 he decided to install a telephone, and as a consequence, telegraph wires were stretched across the river on to the Buckinghamshire bank. These were found to be low enough to annoy the passing bargemen and after many complaints the court ordered that they be raised to a height of 30ft. In November 1875, Lord Otto received permission to erect a waterwheel on the riverbank. This was in position for at least twenty years, but seems to have disappeared without record. When he died in 1883 the estate passed to his widow, Lady Fitzgerald, who sold it in 1895 to John Lewis Phipps. His was a short reign as by 1900 it was in the possession of Sir William Beilby Avery, of Avery Scales fame. Sir William had apparently bought the house to be near the royalty at Windsor, and held many garden parties in the hope of attracting them. Whether he was successful is not known, but many ladies and gentlemen of quality attended the parties, for which Sir William always engaged the Brigade of Guards band from Windsor barracks.

Sir William died in 1908 and Lady Avery continued living at the Court until 1916 when she sold it to Ernest Olivier of the Olivier Shipping Company, who paid £27,000 for the building plus fifty acres of woodland. During his lifetime he spent a further £20,000 on improvements to the Court. Mr Olivier was born of French parents in Ismir, Turkey, and was described as a businessman, diplomat and public benefactor. For six months of the year he lived in Monte Carlo, where he acted in an honorary capacity as Turkish Consul. He frequently entertained ambassadors and diplomats at Oakley Court, and as a courteous gesture flew the flag of the nation they represented. During the Second World War, General de Gaulle was a frequent visitor, and it may be for this reason that it has been said that Oakley Court was used as the English headquarters of the French Resistance.

Ernest Olivier lived at Oakley Court until his death in 1965, when he was 100 years old. For the next fourteen years the building was deserted and allowed to crumble and fall into disrepair by its absentee owners. At a later date, a secret vault was discovered on the ground floor of the building and found to contain papers and documents relating to the Olivier family, dating from 1910–35.

In 1950 Hammer Films took over Down Place, next door to Oakley Court, and turned it into Bray Studios. The close proximity of the court to the studios, plus the fact that it took on a sinister Gothic appearance, eventually led to it being used as a location for a number of films, including *Half a Sixpence* with Tommy Steele, *Murder by Death* with Peter Sellers, and the light-hearted *St Trinians* series, where the Court was home for 100 delinquent schoolgirls.

In 1957 Hammer Films found its true vocation when it started to make modern versions of the classic horror stories, including those featuring Dracula, Frankenstein and the Wolf Man, mainly starring Christopher Lee and Peter Cushing. Oakley Court became 'Dracula's Castle', and was seen by millions as the home of the world's most famous vampire. To obtain an eerie effect, the directors used only candles to light the entire Court.

In 1979 the crumbling mansion was put on the market by the trustees of the Olivier family, and was purchased by the present owners who converted it into the hotel we see today. Two wings were added onto the main house, the River Block and the Garden Block, which together housed eighty-four extra bedrooms. Under the direction of Nicholas Galitzine, a workforce of thirty men carried out renovation to all the wood and furniture and installed 200 beds and 10,000 sq yards of carpeting. The project, when complete, cost £5 million.

The Oakley Court Hotel opened on 7 November 1981 under the first manager, Geoffrey Tucker, who had previously run the Colony Club in Barbados. The following year the architects, Nellist, Blundell & Flint of Ealing, were given a special commendation by the Maidenhead Civic Society for their restoration of the interior of the Court. Also in 1982, the Duke of Edinburgh was guest of honour at a special dinner given to commemorate the connection between the Court and Dracula, its most notorious occupant. Before the meal the guests were given blood orange cocktails and garlic vodka. The first courses were black caviar and blood sausages, followed by the main course of filet Marie Louise a la Club 41, which referred to the vampire's girlfriend. The sweet was Transylvanian nut torte, washed down with bulls' blood wine. Today, with its former splendour and beautiful setting of thirty-five acres of landscaped gardens on the banks of the Thames, Oakley Court ranks as one of the county's outstanding landmarks.

Down Place, home of the Kit Kat Club.

Down Place

Down Place, now better known as Bray Studios, is situated on the river bank next door to Oakley Court. The architecture of the house dates to 1750, which was undoubtedly a period of major alterations. The origins, however, may lie in the fifteenth century, as in 1518 the house passed to Sir Robert Jones. After his death in 1552 he left the property to his heir, David, and his widow, Katherine.

By 1600 it was in the hands of the Page family, who owned considerable tracts of land in the area, including that on which Oakley Court now stands. Arthur Page died in 1610 leaving it to his brother, Randolph. By 1627, John Page was the owner and in that year he leased it to Richard and Henry Powney.

In 1720 the mansion was bought by Jacob Tonson, a publisher and bookseller of some fame. At Down Place he held regular meetings of the Kit Kat Club, which purported to be a gathering of 'men of wit and pleasure about town'. The members included the Earl of Dorset, the Duke of Marlborough and Lord Halifax, together with many other noblemen and gentlemen. Writers of the day, like Addison and Steele, frequented the meetings, and even the poets Alexander Pope and Dryden were involved. But beneath the facade of literary joviality the club had more sinister objectives, concerned with the defence of the House of Hanover. The political movement undoubtedly had its origins in the Glorious Revolution of 1688, but the club itself was founded in 1700 by Jacob Tonson, who was the first elected secretary. The initial meetings took place at the Cat & Fiddle, Shire Lane, London. The landlord, one Christopher Cat, who gave his name to the club, served the members with mutton pies.

At that time, the Whigs foresaw that after the death of William III there might be a serious danger of a Jacobite movement, calculated to imperil the Protestant succession. The club met more frequently and after William's death in 1705, Tonson bought a house at Barn Elms and built a special room for the meetings. When he moved to Down Place thirteen years later, he built a similar room which was still in use after his death in 1756. During the early days of the club, Sir Godfrey Kneller had painted portraits of fifteen of the members, and these were hung in Down Place until 1772, when Richard, the last of the Tonson dynasty, and MP for Windsor, died. After the Tonsons the house passed to the Duke of Argyle, and then to Baker Church and John Huddlestone, all in the space of fifty years. In 1807 Henry Harford bought the estate and his family held it until 1955, when it was purchased by George Davis.

Hammer Films moved into the old mansion in 1950. A series of stages and outbuildings were added and film sets erected on the spot. The first film made at Bray was *Cloudburst* and this was followed by a series of modest thrillers during the years 1951-56, which culminated in the very successful *Quatermass* films bringing new dimensions in horror.

Realising the market potential, Hammer changed their policy in 1957 and embarked on remakes of the classic horror films, bringing a sense of realism to the old stories. Tomato ketchup ran freely at Down Place when they made the *Dracula* and *Frankenstein* series, and featured other old favorites like *The Mummy* and *The Wolf Man*. By 1968, when they had finished filming, there were not too many horrific stories left unfilmed.

Down Place is still part of Bray Studios, which nowadays provides various services to the film and television industries, including commercials and pop videos. In its lifetime the old house has entertained both gentry and film stars, with personalities as diverse as the Duke of Marlborough, Christopher Lee and Errol Flynn.

Monkey Island

Monkey Island is situated in the River Thames, some half a mile from Bray Lock on the stretch to Boveney and Windsor. It is presently the site of a hotel and can be reached either from Bray Village or from Builders Cross on the A308 road from Maidenhead to Windsor. It is joined to the riverbank by a bridge erected in 1956; before that it was only accessible by boat or ferry. The island lies in the ancient royal manor and parish of Bray, founded in Anglo-Saxon times when the boundaries were laid out. The royal associations date back to AD 942 when King Edmund I governed the area from his palace in Old Windsor. The connection continued after Windsor Castle became the royal residence in 1110, and Bray became a dormitory area to house the officials of the King's court. The lands at Bray, including the islands in the Thames, normally formed a

Picnicking on Monkey Island in the nineteenth century.

part of the Queen's dowry, but were often leased out to suitable users. Bray lay on the edge of the Windsor Forest, a vast area with a circumference of seventy-seven miles which was used by the Kings as a hunting ground. Oaks from the forest were used for the building of local bridges and were often loaded onto barges at Queen's Wharf, just downriver from Monkey Island. One document of 1535 records that 'the Bishop of Winchester shipped quantities of oak from his estate at Billingbear in Windsor Forest from Water Oakley'. The name Oakley denotes a clearing in an oak wood.

The island came into being around 10,000 BC, at the end of a series of ice ages. The Thames Valley itself was carved from the chalk to a depth of 150ft over a period of around half a million years, during which time the fast-flowing torrent of melting ice washed away the surface deposits. During inter-glacial periods, when the river was more stable, a series of flood plains were formed on which hunter-gatherers of the Old Stone Age made their settlements. No evidence of prehistoric occupation has been located on Monkey Island, probably due to the overburden of soil that was placed on the island during the late medieval period. However, sites of these early Thames settlers have been located close by where gravel extraction has taken place adjacent to Monkey Island Lane. In 1991, a Bronze Age farming community dating to 1,000 BC was excavated at the nearby Weir Bank Farm, with round houses and granaries. In the nineteenth century, Monkey Island Lane was known as Arbour Lane, and was a Roman road leading from Bray village to Water Oakley where a Roman settlement and burial ground were located. The name Arbour derives from 'Ere-burgh' meaning 'the former town'. From the ninth to the eleventh centuries, anyone standing on Monkey Island would have witnessed the Danish longships making their way up river as far as Oxford on their numerous raids. In AD 851 the *Anglo-Saxon Chronicles* recorded that the Danes were defeated by King Ethelwulf at the site of Acleah, which can be identified with Oakley, one quarter of a mile downriver from Monkey Island. It was during the late Anglo-Saxon or the early Norman period that Monkey Island received its name. It is popularly assumed that the island takes its name from the famous monkey paintings which can be seen in one of the hotel buildings, but it actually derives from the earlier title of 'Monks-Eyot', suggesting that it was originally land being used by monks, perhaps close to their fishery in the Thames.

The monks in question resided in the moated site of Amerden Bank, Taplow, close by Bray Lock. This building became a cell of Merton Priory in the year 1197 when William de Turville leased the site to the prior. It was described at this time as 'three virgates and two acres and an assail with fishing in the Thames'. The mentioned assart probably referred to Monkey Island. Domesday evidence suggests that before the Norman Conquest, Amerden was held by Stigand, the deposed Archbishop of Canterbury, which may mean that the island was used by monks in Anglo-Saxon times. A series of fishponds on the island may date back to this period. By 1361 the Bray Courts Rolls record that the island was called Bournhames Eyte, in a document entitling John Casse and John Tyelhurst to use it for pasturage at a charge of 2*s* 6*d* per annum. The name occurs again in a Public Record Office plan of 1640 when it is referred to as Burnham Ayt. Presumably before the Dissolution the island was in the hands of Burnham Abbey. The abbey, which stands close by on the Buckinghamshire bank, was a house of Augustinian canonesses founded by Richard, Earl of Cornwall, on 18 April 1266. From the late twelfth century, the island belonged to the manor of Earley Whiteknights, now the site of Reading University, who probably leased it to the monks. The White Knight himself was John de Earley, who died in 1324. In 1606 the island passed to the Englefield family who held it until 1738.

After the Great Fire of London in 1666, which destroyed a large area of the City, large quantities of Berkshire stone were shipped to the capital for rebuilding, and on the return journey the barges were laden with unwanted rubble which was dumped on islands in the Thames. Monkey Island got its fair share of rubble which proved to be a blessing in disguise. Not only did it raise the level sufficiently to make the island immune from the worst floods, but it provided a solid foundation for building. In 1738 Sir Francis Englefield sold the island to Charles Spencer, the third Duke of Marlborough. Charles Spencer succeeded his brother as the fifth Earl of Sunderland in 1729 and inherited the dukedom on the death of his aunt, Henrietta in 1733. The duke was an inveterate gambler and an addicted sportsman, and was always in debt. This did not please Sarah, Dowager Duchess of Marlborough, who was annoyed by his spendthrift ways and by his marriage in 1732 to Elizabeth Trevor, whom she regarded as a simple woman. During his lifetime she did her best to ensure that the duke did not inherit Blenheim Palace.

However, on her death in 1744, the palace, together with the considerable income from its estate, passed to Charles Spencer. Before that date he had been forced to occupy a lodge in Windsor Great Park, and it was while he was living there, and attending the notorious Kit Kat Club at nearby Down Place, that he first saw Monkey Island. The duke

The Monkey Island temple, before the hotel was built.

inherited Blenheim in 1744, and it was at this time that he decided to use some of his newly-acquired resources to build two lodges on Monkey Island as a sporting retreat from both London and Blenheim. Despite his reputation as a spendthrift, the trustees of the late duchess did not object to this expenditure. For the building scheme, the duke chose the Palladian architect Roger Morris, who had worked for him on two previous occasions. In 1732 he had built the stables and Gardener's House at Althorp, and in 1738 he had erected other stables for use of the 2nd troop of Horse Guards in Park Street, Mayfair. Previously Morris had been blacklisted by the duchess for not complying with her demands when erecting a house for her in Wimbledon in 1731. Clearly the duke thought differently about Morris's talents. The cost of the buildings on Monkey Island was high, and a total of £8,756 was paid for the creation of the banqueting house and fishing lodge. In addition to this the ninth Earl of Pembroke, who was acting as Morris's architectural consultant, put in a bill for £2,277 for his work during the years 1745 to 1748. Payments to Morris and Pembroke, however, ceased abruptly in 1748 due to the state of the duke's finances. By the time of his death in 1749, Roger Morris had only received £2,707 of the total, and the remainder was paid in instalments to his executor, Robert Andrews, until November 1755. The original estimate had enabled Morris to have his most skilled craftsmen, including his own son, James, experienced mason George Mercer, and the renowned carver William Perritt.

Lady Hertford visited the island soon after the completion of the buildings and was suitably unimpressed when she wrote:

> He has a small house upon it, whose outside represents a farm, the inside what you please; for the parlour, which is the only room in it except a kitchen, is painted upon the ceiling in grotesque, with monkeys, fishing, shooting, etc and its sides are hung with paper. When a person sits in this room he cannot see the water, though the island is not above a stone's cast over: nor is he prevented from this by shade; for, except for six or eight walnut trees and a few orange trees in tubs, there is not a leaf upon the island; it arises entirely from the river running very much below its banks. There is another building which I think is called a temple… It should seem that his Grace has taken a hint from the Man of Ross's public spirit; and in order not to copy him too slavishly, has bestowed a treat upon the eyes instead of the bellies of the passengers.

Similarly, in 1748 Lady Newdigate visited and wrote that Marlborough had spent £8,000 on 'only two disagreeable buildings, one of which consists of a parlour and a kitchen, ye parlour painted all over with monkeys'.

The original buildings, as erected by Charles Spencer, consisted of an octagonal fishing lodge and a temple or banqueting pavilion. The lodge was of two storeys, of which the upper was the duke's bedroom. It was built entirely of wooden blocks which were made to look like cut stone, and as such was a monument of the craftsmanship of 200 years ago. The style is Palladian with a Diocletian window on each face. The building is reminiscent of another octagonal construction adjacent to Carne's Seat in the grounds of Goodwood House, also thought to have been designed by Roger Morris. Perhaps the most significant feature of the lodge are the monkey paintings which adorn the splayed ceiling. These were completed by the French artist Clermont, sometimes known as Francois and at other times Andien. They are classified as singeries, a French word meaning to ape or mimic, and to this end Clermont has featured monkeys instead of people involved in various sports. Given Marlborough's passion for sport, this is perhaps not surprising. Many of the panels feature the monkeys shooting, punting and fishing, all activities carried out by the duke himself. The scenes are distinctly surreal in approach, and one panel features a monkey harpooning a dolphin, while the ceiling depicts monkeys sitting in a shell hauled by two more dolphins, with another serenading them from afar with a conch shell. The latter panel parodies Raphael's *Triumph of Galatea* and Caracci's *Galatea*, whilst other panels feature classical legends like Narcissus, and Leda and the Swan. The paintings at Monkey Island were restored in 1987 by Piotz Koneczny.

The temple, or banqueting pavilion, was square with projections and was built of stone in two storeys. The ground floor was originally open like a market hall. The upper room, once used as a billiard room, has a magnificent stucco ceiling with Neptune, mermaids, shells, water sprites and other figures in high relief plaster work. The design of the building suggests the involvement of the Earl of Pembroke and has similarities with the Water House at Houghton Hall, Norfolk, designed by Pembroke in 1730. William Perritt was probably responsible for the elaborate heavy mouldings in the Wedgewood Room. Both the lodge and the temple are Grade I listed buildings.

By the early nineteenth century the two main structures were surrounded by an array of outbuildings, and these were still there when the lodge was turned into a hostelry in 1840. At first it was probably a simple alehouse or inn rather than a hotel and the earliest recorded host appears to be James Franklin, mentioned in 1854 as a victualler. He seems to have managed the hostel until at least 1873 when Robert Plummer, also recorded as a fisherman, appears to have taken over. The Plummers ran the business until the end of the century, and Mrs Plummer was noted for her excellent cooking. It is recorded that Eton Excelsior Rowing Club opened its season in 1892 by 'proceeding to Monkey Island where they partook of their annual spread at Host Plummer's', which infers that they used the inn regularly.

The actual date when Monkey Island became a hotel cannot be determined with accuracy, but it was probably during the time when the Plummers were hosts. The demand for hotels began in the 1880s when the Thames became a pleasure ground, whereas in 1870 pleasure craft were few and far between. During the 1880s indecent bathers were prosecuted on Monkey Island, which may infer that activities on the island were at a minimum.

In 1893 there were ferries crossing both from Bray and the Bucks bank at Dorney. Several punts were kept for ferrying wood, coal, stones and visitors. One Irish ferryman, who rowed visitors across before the bridge was built in 1956, expected a glass of Guinness every twenty minutes, and if the drinks were not forthcoming, he would take the boat back to shore and leave the visitors behind! There is an unconfirmed report that George III lived on the island for a period just before his death, with a monkey as a pet, but this may be a myth associated with the name of the island. However, at some time during the hotel's history a monkey named Jacko was chained to a walnut tree in an attempt to promote the establishment. He apparently escaped and so terrified a pregnant woman in Bray that her son was stillborn.

During the 1900s, the Thames was being used regularly by pleasure seekers and there were 11,284 rowing boats and 541 steam launches registered for use on the river. By 1903, the hotel had been taken over by Thomas Wiltshire and he was superseded in 1911 by James Balfour. By the time of the First World War, John Herbert Tinker was the host and he held it until 1923. In the Edwardian era Monkey Island Hotel became a very fashionable place to visit and attracted royal favour. The Prince of Wales, later Edward VII, and Queen Alexandra regularly had tea on the lawns whilst visiting Windsor. They were often surrounded by their children and grandchildren, of whom three were future Kings.

Another visitor to the island at this time was Edward Elgar, who composed his violin concerto in the house called the Hut on the riverside facing the hotel in 1910. He stayed there as a guest of the Schuster family, as did Clara Butt and Nellie Melba, famous singers of their time. Later, the Hut was renamed the Long White Cloud and was the home of racing driver Stirling Moss, who brought his friends across to dine at the hotel. From 1913 to 1923, Monkey Island was a love nest for authors H.G. Wells and Rebecca West. At forty-six, Wells was already an established writer, whilst Rebecca at twenty had still to bring out her first book. When she eventually published *The*

King Edward VII and family taking tea on Monkey Island.

Return of the Soldier in 1918, her hero was to fall in love with the daughter of the host of the Monkey Island Inn, which resembled her own affair with Wells. In the third chapter of the novel, she describes the island as follows:

> In front were the dark green glassy waters of an unvisited backwater, and beyond then a bright lawn set with many walnut trees and a few great chestnuts, well lit with their candles, and to the left of that a low white house with a green dome rising in its middle and a verandah whose roof of hammered iron had gone verdigris colour with age and the Thames weather. This was the Monkey Island Inn. The third Duke of Marlborough had built it for a 'folly' and perching there with nothing but a line of walnut trees and a fringe of lawn between it and the fast full shining Thames it had a grace and silliness that belonged to the eighteenth century.

There was no doubt that both Wells and Rebecca considered Monkey Island to be a magical place, as well as a haven away from the wagging tongues. When in May 1916 Rebecca booked in at the Riviera Hotel, Maidenhead, and suggested that Wells joined her there, she received the following exasperated reply:

> I wanted you to go to Monkey Island. I could have come there. The Riviera is quite impossible for me – so I suppose we must now consider ourselves separated until you get to Hatch End. It is a bore. But I can't risk our being seen in sin at that conspicuous place next door to Murray's. Baerlein's appearance I think settled that conclusively. Monkey Island would have been cheaper, cleaner, safer and I wanted it. I hope you may presently

> muddle through to some sort of possible arrangement. For two years we have muddled, been uncomfortable and piled up expenditure, your output of work has been trivial, my work has suffered enormously… From the Riviera I think you had better come up to the Savoy. All of which is just cursing.

Wells' stormy romance with Rebecca ended in 1923, although he may have continued to visit the hotel. He had known Monkey Island since his schooldays when he used to stay with his uncle, Tom Pennicott, at Surly Hall Inn, located half a mile downriver.

In 1928, L.O. Schofield took over the hotel, followed by Malachi McGarry in 1931, who held it well into the Second World War. Later in the 1950s, when Christopher Reynolds was the host, a long, low block of stripped-classical style was built adjoining the banqueting house. In 1963 major alterations took place when the dining area of the hotel was increased by the addition of a large glass-sided building which included a tree and a fishpool. In 1970 the Marlborough Room was added at the upstream end, which had walls decorated with battle scenes. In the same year the temple was extended to provide twenty-five extra bedrooms. In 1986 the then owner, Major Fitzwilliams, sold the island to Mr Basil Faidi, who in 1987 consulted English Heritage over the restoration of the buildings. At this time, Piotz Koneczny was engaged to restore the monkey paintings. Beneath the surface of the lawn lies an area once cultivated by the medieval monks and the charred remains of London buildings destroyed by fire in 1666. On the surface, Canada geese wander among the ornamental flowerbeds, swans nest, and peacocks cry and display in an idyllic setting. There is no doubt that Monkey Island is a magical place.

Chapter Five

Waltham and Shottesbrooke

The Church of St Mary the Virgin has a very early foundation, but despite this has been very much ignored by historians in the past, who have recorded little of its history, and preferred to concentrate on the neighbouring churches of Shottesbrooke and Waltham St Lawrence. At one time all three buildings were situated in the Saxon province of Wealdham, which was later broken up into the three separate parishes. We have evidence that there was a church at White Waltham in Saxon times, administered by the Abbey of Chertsey. In the Domesday entry this is translated from the Latin as a small church which probably describes a chapel of which the incumbent was a canon from Chertsey. As the land was being used to provide household supplies for the abbey, it is likely that the chapel was built as a place of worship for the monks and itinerant workers on the estate. As such, it was probably only used at certain times. In contrast to Shottesbrooke, it is unlikely to have adopted parish church status before AD 1100. In true Saxon style it would undoubtedly have been a small wooden building, perhaps situated on the site of the present chancel. The Thorold mentioned at Domesday as holding 150 acres from the abbot, may conceivably have been the same Thorold the Priest who held the church at West Hannay, Berkshire, at this time. In this case he would be the earliest named incumbent. Several low-level graves discovered accidentally over the years in the churchyard may relate to this period.

The history of the present building has to some extent been obscured by the restoration which took place in 1868 when, apart from the chancel, the majority of the church was rebuilt. Two twelfth-century arches at the west end of the church however are evidence of an early Norman rebuilding, and the amount of thirteenth century work indicates that there was a substantial extension made at this time.

The pleasant churchyard has the usual variety of gravestones illustrating the history of the parishioners. To the east of the entrance gate is an interesting path made up of what appear to be memorial stones, inscribed with initials and date only. These are footstones associated with graves situated on the north side of the church. Outside the churchyard, beside the road, is a set of old stocks and a whipping post dating from the seventeenth century. These have now been partly restored.

White Waltham Church.

White Waltham Church and the stocks.

The earliest mention of the lands of Waltham occurs in AD 940 when King Edmund granted thirty hides at Wealdham to the thegn Aelfsige. This area, representing 3,600 acres, covered the three settlements of White Waltham, Shottesbrooke and Waltham St Lawrence, and is very close to the assessment of twenty-six hides listed as four entries in the *Domesday Book*. It would seem that during the early Anglo-Saxon period Wealdham, as it was then called, was one large royal estate situated in the ancient Forest of Windsor. Part of the discrepancy of two hides is probably represented by the twelve strips of meadow outside the bounds mentioned in the charter and located near Strande Water at Cookham. The name derives from the two elements; 'Weald' (woodland) and 'Ham' (enclosure) and is usually associated with early Saxon forest clearance between the years AD 450-550. The element 'Weald' always becomes 'Walt' by the eleventh century, and the study of other Waltham names indicates that they were usually administrative centres associated with royalty and hunting. In this case, the royal estate and forest belonged to the castle and palace at Windsor. Most Wealdhams have also produced evidence of Roman remains, and these are represented by the Romano-British temple and associated settlement in Weycock Field, Waltham St Lawrence, which are situated on the Camlet Way, the Roman road from St Albans to Silchester.

The charter of around AD 940 provides early evidence of some of the landmarks in the three parishes, which exist as boundary markers. These include Wulla Leage (Woolley Green), Hild Leah (Littlewick), Weg Cocce (Weycock Field), Hwitan Pearruc (White Paddock), Heal Wicum (Hallwick Wood) and Wassanhamme (Smewyns Moat). Use of the word 'Leah' in the northern part suggests clearing and settlement in this area, while the southern section was made up of marsh (hamme) and forest.

By the year 1007, Shottesbrooke had been carved out of the original estate of Wealdham, and it can be assumed that White Waltham and Waltham St Lawrence had become manors in their own right. By around 1060 White Waltham as we know it today had been divided up into two estates. The largest portion, an area of ten hides, was granted with the chapel of the parish by King Edward the Confessor to the Abbot of Chertsey for the household supplies of the monks, and the lands included the woods at Hallwick, near Brick Bridge, Littlewick and Southwode.

After the Norman Conquest, Chertsey Abbey, which had been founded in AD 666, continued to hold the land and the *Domesday Book* records that there was enough for twelve ploughs, together with nine acres of meadow and enough woodland to feed five pigs on acorns and beech mast for one year. There was a population of around seventy-two, not including the monks, and one slave. A man called Thorold held 160 acres from the abbot, and on his land he had two ploughs and two cottages. The value of the settle was £8.

The other estate, a smaller area of three hides, was represented by the present settlement of Woodlands Park, with lands stretching over to Paley Street. In the early eleventh century it was owned by Harold, Earl of Wessex, who died not long into his reign at the Battle of Hastings in 1066. He founded the Abbey of Waltham Cross in the year 1060 and endowed the monastery with many of his landholdings, including his estate at White Waltham.

In 1066 the land was being administered by Canon Wulfwin, but was given by William I at Domesday to the Bishop of Durham. However, Waltham Abbey continued to lease it from the bishop.

The Domesday entry tells us that the lay population was forty-four with three slaves, with land for six ploughs, three acres of meadow, woodland for six pigs and a value of 100*s*.

Medieval documents refer to the Waltham Abbey holding as both West Waltham and Herwode Waltham. As the land is clearly not situated to the west of White Waltham parish, the first name probably derives from the fact that it was the most westerly landholding of the abbey. The second name, which later became Heywood, is believed to be a corruption of Harold's Wood, referring to the Saxon owner.

During his reign, Henry II (1154-89) confirmed the lands at West Waltham to the canons, and Richard I (1189-99) granted them the liberty to enclose their woods at Heywood and White Paddock with a hedge and ditch. In a charter of 1227 the canons received licence to take hare, fox and cat at West Waltham.

By the thirteenth century the whole settlement took on the name of Whyte Waltham and in an assize roll of 1283 is described as the 'vill of Blaunche Walthem', from the Norman dialect. The prefix 'white', as both names indicate, is presumed to allude to the fact that the parish stands on the edge of the chalk.

The abbots continued to rule the roost, as evidenced by the Hundred Rolls of 1274, which records that the present Abbot of Waltham had erected gallows in Heywode commencing with this year and has hanged there a certain woman contrary to the liberty of the lord, King and without warrant. The Abbot of Chertsey claims to have the same warrant. It is interesting to note that the Abbot of Waltham in question was one Reginald de Maidenheth, who had been appointed in 1274. He obviously had some connection with Maidenhead as did his successor Robert de Elenton, elected on Christmas Day 1289.

The thirteenth century saw the formation of additional manors by subinfeudation. Part of the Chertsey Abbey holding was taken at Littlewick to form the manor of Wolvfynnes for Reginald le Forester in 1263. This was later known as Woolley and Feens and perpetuates in the names Woolley Green and Feens Farm. Another created manor was that of Smewyns, situated on the site of the present farmhouse. The Smewyn family were tenants of the parish from a very early date, Roger Smewyn being a witness to an agreement between the Abbot of Waltham and William Cumin, rector of White Waltham, in 1187.

A further manor created from Chertsey land in the fifteenth century was Windsors or Waltham Place, with its manor house located on the hill above the church. The earliest known tenant, one Roger Waltham, had clearly taken his name from the settlement. The two abbeys continued to hold land until the Dissolution. In 1537 the Chertsey estate was granted to Thomas and Cecilia Weldon and became the manor of Bury with its centre and manor house close by the church. The Waltham Abbey lands passed to John Norreys of Fyfield in 1541 and were renamed the manor of West Waltham or Heywoods.

By 1633 this manor was held by the Sawyer family, whose residence was Heywood Lodge, a three-storey brick building situated at Heywood Park, the earlier name for the settlement of Woodlands Park.

Difficult as it is to visualise a mansion with a front garden planted with tall trees standing on the site of the former Woolworths branch in Maidenhead High Street, it is probably even more difficult to believe that around 1800 this building was transplanted, brick by brick, from its original site in White Waltham. The story of Monkendons reads like a Grimm fairytale. It was first erected opposite the vicarage at White Waltham in 1777 by James Payn, town clerk of Maidenhead. The majority of the materials used to build this Georgian mansion came from the Maidenhead Guildhall, demolished in that year, purchased by Mr Payn for the sum of £100.

James Payn was appointed county treasurer in 1719 and court recorder for Maidenhead in 1800, a position he held until his death in 1822. With such a busy life he found the journeys to work very arduous, and expressed a desire to live in town. He was loath, however, to leave Monkendons as he had built the home to his own specifications.

One night, when he was with a party of his gambling friends, they agreed that if they lost that evening they would shift his mansion, lock, stock and barrel, from where it stood onto a site in Maidenhead of which James Payn had taken possession. This site was where the presently-empty Woolworths now stands. His friends lost their bet and accordingly, as gentlemen of honour, they paid for the house to be dismantled brick by brick and rebuilt in Maidenhead High Street. Even the stone pillars from the gateway were moved, together with the lantern and bright green copper cupola from the roof. A legal document was drawn up for the procedure, which is said to still be in existence.

After the death of James Payn, Monkendons was taken over as a residence and dispensary by Dr Samuel Plumbe and Dr Benjamin Sellis. The latter was Mayor of Maidenhead in 1847, 1860, and 1861. Subsequently Dr Montgomery and his son joined the practice, which transferred to Claremont, Castle Hill, in 1918. The property was taken over in turn by Muklins & Paul, the lawyer Henry Cooper, the town surveyor and R. Clifton Davey, the architect. By 1922 it was a depository for J.C. Webber & Sons.

But why the name Monkendons, you might ask? Research shows that James Payn named his mansion after a much older estate. A tablet in Cookham Church records that one Ralph Pool gave £10 yearly out of the proceeds of an estate called Monkendons, and it is known that Mr Payn distributed bread from his home to the value of this charity which was already in existence. The date can be taken back further when we find that the Annesley family, who came to the area from Nottingham, held Monkendons in the sixteenth century. It features in the wills of Henry Annesley in 1546 and his son, another Henry, in 1601. But the final clue comes from a memorial brass in Cookham Church, recording the death of John Monkenden and his wife Margaret in 1603. This proves that there was a family of that name in the district and that the estate of Monkendons, and ultimately James Payn's mansion, were named after them.

Residents of Woodlands Park and Cox Green were seething over plans for a development of 128 houses at Cannon Lane in the late 1940s, but the project was small scale compared to plans fifty years ago to build a town larger than Maidenhead at White Waltham. It was in 1944, near the end of the Second World War, that it became necessary to relieve the blitzed areas of London of 383,000 of its inhabitants. At this time the Abercromby Plan for Greater London dictated that eight satellite towns were to be built around the capital to house this surplus population. Each town was to house between 25,000 and 60,000 people. White Waltham was chosen as the site of one of these satellite towns, and was expected to accommodate 60,000 inhabitants, many from the overcrowded areas of Acton and Southall. The town was planned to be three miles across, and was to stretch from Waltham St Lawrence to Touchen End and from Woodlands Park to Shurlock Row. Great Wood, the contentious area selected as a site for motorway services, was in the centre of the settlement and it would have been completely wiped out, as indeed would have been the case for ancient villages like Shottesbrook. Waltham Airfield would have become a civil airport, and adjacent fields would have been turned into an industrial zone. This was in an effort to regroup

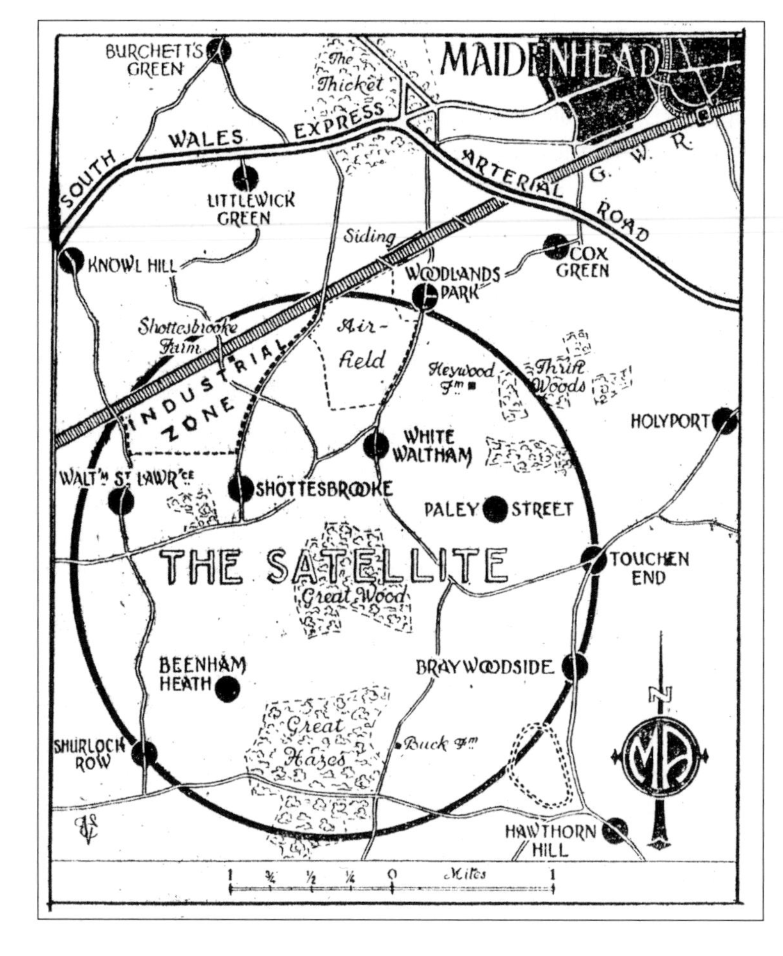

Original plan to build a new town at Waltham.

a large proportion of London's industries and provide work for the new population. Apart from these modern trading estates, the town would be provided with shops, cinemas, churches, schools and cultural facilities.

Construction work was expected to take ten years. A new railway station was to be built in Waltham sidings, and the plan was to electrify the Great Western line between Paddington and Didcot and the Wycombe Branch Line from Maidenhead station. This latter single-track line was to be duplicated.

Construction of the Maidenhead bypass, now represented by the A404M, had begun in 1939, and the plan was to extend it along the A4 as part of an Express Arterial Road between London and South Wales. As we all know, this was the basis of the M4, which was not completed until the 1970s. This bold plan threw the Maidenhead town council and other parish councils into confusion, but they were virtually powerless to act as it was a directive from the Ministry of Town and Country Planning. Fortunately for everybody, it was decided to drop the idea and develop Bracknell instead. Those who can recall how Bracknell has grown since 1948 can probably visualise how the new satellite town would have looked like. So what's new?

White Waltham Airfield

Unlike the Maidenhead Aerodrome that disappeared into the mists after only a few months of operation, White Waltham Airfield has now been in use for nearly seventy-five years. It has also been instrumental in the progress of aviation. The history of the airfield is very extensive and can only be summarised here. More information can be found at the Maidenhead Heritage Centre.

The airfield opened in November 1935 on land purchased from the Dafforn family and Miss Nancy Oswald Smith of the Shottesbrooke estate. Under a government contract, De Havillands constructed buildings on the site and opened a flying school to train pilots for the Royal Air Force Reserve. They first flew Tiger Moths and later graduated to Hawker Audax and Harts. Mr J.M. Cox, who lived in Altwood Bailey during the war years, has cause to remember this early period well as his father, Flight Lieutenant Monty Cox, was Chief Flying Instructor for De Havillands from 1935 until the outbreak of war. During this period, 500 pupils were taught to fly.

At the outbreak of war, the school was renamed Elementary Flying Training School No.13 with a large fleet of DH82A Tiger Moths, with the addition of Ansons, Audax and Harts. Back in 1937 the government had purchased another seventy acres of land, with a view to building an aircraft factory on the site and providing 4,000 jobs in the area. This scheme, however, did not come to fruition and the factory was instead built in Lancashire. The Air Transport Auxiliary (ATA) was formed, and by February 1940 White Waltham had become its headquarters, with Gerard D'Erlanger as the Commanding Office. ATA's No.1 Ferry Pilots Pool was also based at White Waltham.

The purpose of the ATA was to provide civilian pilots to ferry new aircraft from factories to RAF bases and maintenance units, and to transport dispatches, medical supplies and government civilians. To achieve these aims they had their own fleet of Anson and Argus taxi aircraft. This valuable work was carried out until 1945 when the ATA, after holding an air pageant for the public at Waltham, was officially disbanded.

Many Maidonians will remember the hazard of living in close proximity to the airfield during the Second World War. Several aircraft crashed in the vicinity, and bombs intended for the site fell on neighbouring houses. I can remember several such events, and can vividly recall being machine-gunned by a Messerschmitt 109 intent on using up its ammunition.

In July 1940 a German Dornier aircraft dropped seventeen bombs on the airfield, destroying seven Tiger Moths. During 1943, two pilots were killed over Woodlands Park when their Airspeed Oxfords collided, and on 30 July 1944 a badly shot-up Halifax attempted to make a forced landing and ended up in the railway cutting. Fortunately the crew was rescued before the plane exploded. The airfield was also used throughout the war by the Dutch government-in-exile.

In 1942 De Havilland sold their interest in the airfield to the Secretary of State for Air, and in 1946 the RAF Reserve Command moved back onto the premises. The same year, M.L. Aviation came into being (having been resident at White Waltham during the war as R. Malcolm) and carried out much experimental work covered by the Official Secrets Act. Most of M.L.'s projects concerned aviation aids, and during the war they had invented, among other things, the flying Jeep, the man pick-up and quick-release towing ropes. After the war they developed the inflatable wing and radio-controlled target aircraft.

In 1945 the West London Aero Club was formed by three ex-ATA members, and in 1947 Fairey Aviation and Fairey Air Surveys moved to the site from their premises near Heathrow. Fairey Surveys brought with them the C47 Dakotas that they were using for aerial photography and geographical exploration work.

During their stay at White Waltham, Fairey Aviation developed three main aircraft. The first was the Fairey Gannet, an anti-submarine aircraft for the Royal Navy. The second was the ultra-light helicopter, a two-seater designed for Army observation, a project that was abandoned in 1958. Finally came the Rotodyne, a compound helicopter designed to carry forty-eight civilian passengers. The prototype made its first flight on 6 November 1957, and the future looked promising. When Faireys were taken over by Westlands in February 1960, the major development work on the Rotodyne was transferred to Yeovil. However the project was scrapped in 1962 when government funding was withdrawn. In 1964, Westlands left the airfield altogether.

Fairey Air Surveys, who were not part of the Westlands takeover, continued their aerial survey until 1981. The relief mapping side of the business continued after the premises were moved from the airfield to Maidenhead town centre. The firm later became Clyde Surveys. On 25 November 1982, White Waltham Airfield was sold at an auction in Maidenhead Town Hall by the Property Services Agency on behalf of the Ministry of Defence. Five parties bid for the airfield, and it was finally sold for £500,000 to an unnamed business consortium. Until this auction, White Waltham was the largest grassed airfield in Europe, at 256 acres.

Woodlands Park

Today, Woodlands Park is virtually part of Maidenhead and the terminus of a suburban bus route. Some eighty years ago a concentrated series of gruesome events gave the settlement such a bad reputation that it became necessary to change its name. Prior to 1936, it was known as Heywood Park and had the status of an isolated village in the parish of Waltham. The present village grew up around the edge of the estate and took the name of Heywood Park.

The first recorded gruesome event at Heywoods was in 1275 when Reginald de Maidenheth wrongly hanged a woman on the illegal gallows described earlier. In 1839, when the Great Western Railway was excavated, the site of the gallows was disturbed. As if struck by a curse, the railway began to claim victim after victim. Of the many recorded cases, one of the strangest was that which occurred at Christmas 1905, when Joseph Hussey from Woolwich, apparently in a trance, opened the door of an express train at Waltham sidings and fell onto the rails. Mr Cripps, a local platelayer, discovered his body minus a leg, with belongings which were strewn along the line. His body was taken to the Barley Mow at Cox Green and a verdict of accidental death declared by the coroner.

The Heywood Gallows.

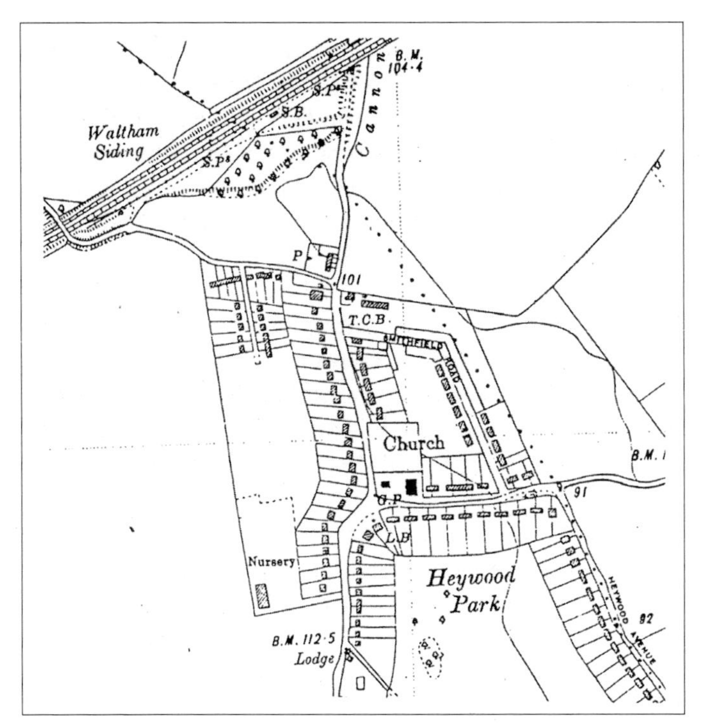

Waltham siding and Heywood Park.

In January 1913, at the same spot, ganger Henry White found the decapitated body of a man who was never identified. A more bizarre story was that of Hilda Craig of Tunbridge Wells, who in June 1929 was found dead on the line with her head and arms severed. The injuries and position of the body were conducive with suicide and she was known to have fits of depression. However, her movements pointed to the fact that she must have alighted from the train at Waltham sidings even though it did not stop. The circumstances remained a mystery.

In October 1930 a platelayer was killed after being struck by a moving train at the fatal spot, and in May 1935 the decapitated body of William Cullinford of Swindon was found after he appeared to fall from a train. He was identified by his son who said he was subject to fainting fits. After deliberation, suicide while of unsound mind was the coroner's verdict.

While these events were happening on the railway, even more gruesome things were occurring in the village. In April 1929, police forced entry into a bungalow after the local milkman, Alexander Kirby, reported seeing a dead woman through the window when making a delivery. In one bedroom the police found the body of Jessie Goldup with her throat cut and her skull fractured by a hammer. Nearby was her husband, who was unconscious, with wounds to the throat. A note written by James Goldup to his mother indicated that he and his wife had decided to die together. Nevertheless at Oxford Assizes, Goldup, a thirty-six-year-old baker, was found insane and ordered to be detained at His Majesty's pleasure, charged with the murder of his wife.

Two more events occurred during 1932. In January Mrs K. Hawkins returned to her home in Breadcroft Lane to find the house locked. When she forced open the front door, she was confronted with gas fumes and her husband's body lying on the floor of the kitchen. The gas pipe had been cut with a hacksaw and Mr Hawkins had laid his head on a pillow. His wife reported that her husband, who was twenty-eight, was unemployed and concerned over his inability to keep a wife and child. The verdict was suicide while of unsound mind.

The second event occurred in September, when the body of Gwendoline Warren, aged thirty-six, was found by a neighbour under a mattress in a house in Heywood Avenue. Mrs Warren had been living with a man named Ernest Hutchinson for two months before the tragedy. He had apparently sold her furniture, taken her jewellery and gone to London to pick up a prostitute, before going with her to Southend. Hutchinson was tracked down, charged with wilful murder, and later hanged in Oxford Jail.

It was at this stage that the name of the settlement was changed to Woodlands Park. By 1935 Messrs Cripps & Green, local builders, had completed forty-six out of an estate of sixty-five semi-detached bungalows in the village, and they were finding it difficult to sell them due to the adverse publicity from the deaths. The builders applied to Mr Frank Bissley, a local landowner, to see if he could bring influence to bear and have the name changed to attract buyers to the estate. Accordingly, the change took place in 1935, with no publicity in the *Maidenhead Advertiser*. Alexander Kirby, the aforementioned milkman, claimed to have suggested the prefix of 'Woodlands' after a small-holding of that name near Marlow.

It is curious to note that with all the tragedies cited, the victims were either from distant places or had moved into Woodlands Park just a few weeks before they died. No residents of the village were involved, and appeared to be immune from the violence. The removal of the word 'Heywood' from the title seemed to have had the desired effect of laying the ghosts of the past to rest, as if an exorcism had taken place. Since that day, Woodlands Park has had no tragic incidents to speak of, with the exception perhaps of an air-taxi plane that crashed on two Smithfield Road bungalows in March 1942, killing three passengers and injuring twenty residents. But that was one of the misfortunes of war.

Ivor Novello

He was born David Ivor Davies over 100 years ago, on 15 January 1893. In 1914, under the name Ivor Novello, he gained immediate fame when he wrote *Keep the Home Fires Burning* to boost the morale of the troops in the First World War.

He went on to become a composer, playwright, actor, film star and producer. He was described as the epitome of romance and glamour, and the darling of the musicals. He was a handsome man who was always surrounded by women, although he never became romantically involved with them and died a bachelor. He changed his name on his birthday in 1927, just ten months before he purchased Munro Lodge

Redroofs at Littlewick Green, home of Ivor Novello.

at Littlewick Green, which was to become his Redroofs home until he died in 1951. The estate included four adjoining cottages where he allowed friends and pensioners to live rent-free. It was here, with his lyricist Christopher Hassell, that he wrote many of his hit musicals which included *Glamorous Night*, *The Dancing Years*, *Perchance To Dream* and *Kings Rhapsody*. He liked nothing better than to relax at Redroofs at weekends and hold house parties for his friends. Each room of the house had a different colour scheme, and many were reserved for specific guests like Constance Collier and Olive Gilbert. His lifelong friend Bobby Andrews had his own quarters, as did his secretary Lloyd Williams, whose room became a locked-up shrine after his death.

Ivor's own bedroom was decorated in grey, silver, blue and red and contained a luxury bed covered with glazed chintz which had been presented to him by film star Joan Crawford. In the gardens were a swimming pool, tennis courts, flower-filled borders and lilac bushes, which inspired him to write the hit song 'We'll Gather Lilacs'.

His mother, Dame Clara Novello Davies, lived with him until her death in 1943. The people of Littlewick regarded him as a good neighbour, and he took part in village activities; he was often seen at the Institute or cricket club. The late Canon Fry, when vicar of Littlewick, regularly gave his opinion on Ivor's new songs. Ivor often provided special local shows on Sundays, and charity matinees at the Rialto Cinema, Maidenhead, with a galaxy of stars from the West End.

His pride and joy was his Rolls-Royce, with his initials on the door panels. During the Second World War he applied for a licence to buy petrol, but was refused on the

Shottesbrooke Church, built in 1337.

grounds that he was not carrying out essential war work. One of his infatuated fans offered him a way out, which turned out to be illegal, and in 1944 he was sentenced to eight weeks in Wormwood Scrubs, despite his fame and popularity.

Ivor often said that he wanted to drop dead after the applause of a first night curtain, preferably before the curtains closed. He was not to achieve this ambition, but passed away peacefully after a weekend house party at Redroofs in March 1951 at the age of fifty-eight.

He left an estate valued at £146,245 and Redroofs was sold to the Actors Benevolent Fund as a home for convalescing stage people. Later it was to become the Redroofs School of Dancing, whose excellent record keeps the memory of Ivor Novello from fading.

Shottesbrooke

The Church of St John the Baptist in Shottesbrooke, which stands in splendid isolation in the grounds of a medieval park, is considered to be a masterpiece of its period. With its tall spire and cruciform plan, it resembles a cathedral in miniature and represents a cross between those at Salisbury and Winchester. It was erected in 1337 and celebrated its 650th anniversary in 1987.

Today Shottesbrooke is a spread-out community consisting mainly of farms and cottages built from the 1900s onwards. The village does not fall into the usual pattern of a compact unit, with the church as a centrepiece, and this has led historians to designate the settlement as a Deserted Medieval Village. The demise of such villages was usually brought about by one of the Black Death in 1349, excessive sheep farming between 1450-1525 or emparkment from the sixteenth to nineteenth centuries. In the case of Shottesbrooke, the latter is likely to be the reason.

To fully understand any relationship between the church and its lost community it is necessary to look into the early history of Shottesbrooke, and here we are fortunate in having records dating back to AD 940. The first clues, however, are in the *Domesday Book* which informs us that there was a church in existence in 1086. This earlier building seems to have been on the same site as the present church; when renovations took place in 1852, the architect U.E. Street reported that 'numerous fragments of Norman buildings and arches were discovered.'

At Domesday, White Waltham only had a chapel belonging to the Abbot of Chertsey, whilst Waltham St Lawrence had a church which had been endowed on the new priory at Hurley by Geoffrey de Mandeville in 1087.

In 1086, Shottesbrooke was situated in a clearing in Windsor Forest and was held by Alward, the King's goldsmith. The population at this time was 106 people, which can be compared with ninety-four in 1801. Most of the inhabitants worked providing charcoal for the refining of the gold used in the manufacture of the King's regalia. This involved cutting down trees from the forest and burning them to form charcoal. It would seem that the gold was also fashioned locally, as in a Pipe Roll of 1166 the settlement is named 'Sotesbroch Aurifabrorum', meaning a work shop with furnaces

Shottesbrooke Lake, created in the seventeenth century.

which used charcoal in the manufacture of gold items. The historian Lysons reported that one King paid 60*s* for regalia at the time of his coronation. The earliest reference to Shottesbrooke is in AD 940, when a grant of thirty hides of land was made by King Eadmund to Aelforsige. In the Domesday entry, Shottesbrooke is quoted as seven hides, so it can be assumed that the grant also included the two Walthams. Later, in 1007, King Aethelread granted eight hides, representing Shottesbrooke only, to Aelfgar. It can be assumed that both Aelfsige and Aelfgar were goldsmiths, together with Alward's father who held the manor in 1066. This would indicate that gold was being fashioned at Shottesbrooke for at least the period AD 940-1166, and probably longer. Although the site of the gold manufactory and the kilns for charcoal burning cannot be pinpointed with certainty, it seems likely that Kiln Hill and the field Kiln Platt, which are located south of Broadmoor Lane, are both associated with the industry. Kiln Platt lies adjacent to Great Wood, which was originally much larger, and this was no doubt the source of the wood for the charcoal. When the Nuffield Ascot pipeline passed through this area, features and large quantities of twelfth and thirteenth-century pottery, together with animal bones and charcoal were found, which seems to substantiate this theory. The moated site at nearby Smewyns Farm, known to be a manor in the Middle Ages, may have been the homestead of the Saxon goldsmiths.

There is a distinct lack of natural sources of water in Shottesbrooke, a commodity necessary for gold refining, as well as the watering of animals. The settlement had a lake in 1283, when an assize roll mentioned the fishing rights of the same, but this was not the same lake seen today, which is known to have been excavated in the seventeenth century to supply materials for extensions to Shottesbrooke Park House.

The most likely site for the original lake is Shottesbrooke Marsh, an area just south of Broadmoor Lane and close to Kiln Platt. An old cottage nearby retains the name 'The Marsh' and the next house along is called 'Marsh Down', indicating a rise in the land. In the charter of AD 940, Smewyns Moat is entitled Wassanhame, which is Anglo-Saxon for 'marsh enclosure'.

Having established that there was a church, a lake, a population and an industry at Shottesbrooke in medieval times, the question arises as to where the lost village of the charcoal burners was sited. We have another clue from an aerial photograph taken in 1963, which shows house platforms as cropmarks in two fields just north of Broadmoor Lane. This was again substantiated by finds of twelfth-century pottery from the pipeline. When added to other features, this forms the image of a compact village and industry sited on each side of Broadmoor Lane, the ancient road linking Windsor to Reading. The manor of Shottesbrooke was in the possession of Ralph le Breton in 1182 and passed to Hugh de Shottesbrooke in 1186. By 1300 it was in the hands of William de Lou, from whom it passed to Reginald dé Pavely in 1310 and to John of Oxonia in 1332. By 1335 it was owned by Sir William Trussell, a knight from Cubblestone, Staffordshire, who was responsible for the erection of the present church as part of a collegiate.

In 1337, Sir William founded a college which was situated to the south of the church. It was administered by a warden with five other chaplains and two clerks, and endowed with the Church of Shottesbrooke and a rental of 40*s* on the manor of the period. On 24 May that year, the founder presented John de Lodyngton to the Bishop of Salisbury as the first warden, and in the following year Edward III granted to Sir William Advowson of the church at Basildon, Berkshire. On 3 June 1341, further endowments were made by the gift of a messuage in Cookham with lands, meadow, weir and rent.

Some time before 1371, the church and college were almost destroyed by fire and all the priests and clerks left, with the exception of John Bradford, the third warden. The penultimate warden was William Throckmorton, who died in 1535, and is buried in the church under his effigy. The last warden was Robert Vere, who was a layman and a brother to the Earl of Oxford. By 1546 the college had been dissolved. None of the buildings stand today, but Thomas Hearne, the White Waltham antiquary, wrote in 1711 of an orchard where all the trees had been shaped into crosses by the monks. In Hearne's time, the college was a farmhouse and he remarks that 'there was a passage from this farmhouse over towards the church way, and so down a pair of steps, by a door, into the south cross of the church'. The blocked-up door of the passage that linked the college to the church can still be seen today in the south wall. As to the college, Hearne describes it as having two spacious halls with their chimneys and parlours.

The Church of St John the Baptist was built in 1337 in the 'Decorated' style. It was erected in the form of a cross with a central tower and spire, a nave, a chancel and north and south transepts. A vestry and a porch were later added to the nave. When the building was finished, legend says that the architect, pleased with his work, climbed to the top of the spire and toasted the completed church with a glass of wine. Unfortunately he lost his balance, fell to his death, and was buried on the spot where he landed. A further tale maintains that the church was completed in a hurry because of the approach of the Black Death.

A gallery and pews were placed in the north transept by Arthur Vansittart in 1722, and further pews added in the south chancel in 1756. On 20 July 1757, the spire was struck by lightning, shattering the roof, destroying the wainscot and the door into the gallery, and breaking the north window. The church was consequently closed for a year and reopened on 24 September 1758 after repairs had been carried out by Townsend of Oxford. The spire was repaired in 1839 by Townsend and yet again in 1844 by Charles Cooper of Maidenhead. There was a general restoration in 1852 under C. Street, an architect who carried out work on many local churches.

Apart from the relatively modern stained glass in the east window, the majority of the fourteenth-century heraldry shields have disappeared. A survey by Peter Begent describes the church as having been ablaze with heraldry, and as many as forty-two shields were seen by Ashmole in 1665. By 1840, when Carlos visited, there were only twelve, and today only six remain. The surviving shields can be dated between 1340-70. Carlos described the east window as having scanty remnants of St John the Evangelist, St John the Baptist, an angel with censer, a Bishop and St Katherine, amongst others.

The monuments in the church are particularly impressive. The largest is the altar tomb to the founder, Sir William Trussell, who died in 1363, and his Lady Maud. This occupies the entire wall of the north transept. In Hearne's time the bodies could be

Shottesbrooke Park House, *c.* 1830.

seen in a defect in the wall, the founder wrapped in lead and his wife in leather at his feet. Their daughter, Margaret, who died in 1401, is buried in the north cross.

On the north wall is the smaller-than-life effigy and tomb of William Throckmorton, the penultimate warden of the college. In a box above him is a key found in the tomb during repairs in 1967, which could conceivably have belonged to one of the doors of the collegiate.

There are numerous other flagstones and monuments, and a very fine collection of brasses. One of these is to Thomas, or Father Noke, who died in 1567. He was a great friend of Henry VIII and obviously shared the same marital habits, if not marital problems, as the brass shows him with his three wives!

The bells in the tower number six in all. Three of these were cast by Ellis Knight of Reading in 1634. The other three were made at the Meals foundry in 1811, 1904 and 1964. A set of Belfry Rules, dated 1900, shows that the ringers were paid for their attendance, but were subject to numerous forfeits if they wore a hat, quarrelled, swore or turned up drunk for duty. On such occasions they usually left the church with the words of the vicar ringing in their ears! After the Dissolution, the college fell into decay but the church remained intact. The manor passed to the De Vere family and then to the Nokes' in 1578. It was held in 1628 by Richard Powle, who sold it to William Cherry in 1698. Robert Vansittart was holding it in 1716 and in 1886 it passed to Mrs Oswald A. Smith. The Smith family have held it ever since, the present owner being the son of John Smith Esquire, a previous High Steward of Maidenhead.

Shottesbrooke Park House is the present manor house and was erected in the sixteenth century, originally on an H-shaped plan with three storeys in the front and two at the back. Early in the nineteenth century an attempt was made to 'gothicise' it with the addition of a stucco-embattled parapet at roof level, hood moulds over the windows, and a portico at the entrance front. Changes to the building have occurred since then and the south-east wing was removed in 1960. A blocked-up door in the church once led from the chancel across the churchyard to this building. Today a sense of peace lies over Shottesbrooke, and the candlelit church, which shares a vicar with White Waltham, is the only ancient reminder of a manor tended by monks. This building stands on the foundations of the Domesday church, which once catered for the goldsmiths and charcoal burners who lived in the parish in Saxon times.

Chapter Six

Thicket and Stubbings

The Thicket, which is administered by the National Trust and listed as 368 acres, is potentially virgin land and has remained undisturbed for at least 1,000 years. Today the Thicket is a haven for birds, animals and wild plants, mainly because large areas are inaccessible, being choked with hawthorn and other fast-growing trees and bushes. The public tend to confine themselves to the footpaths and green rides, which are generally used for picnics and exercising dogs and horses. In 1807, Mavor described it as a waste area and a centre of highway robbery since 1597; in his time it still remained 'a blot on the agriculture of the County although not on its morality'.

Prehistoric earthworks located on the Thicket suggest that at one time the area was not so dense. Victorian antiquaries describe many dubious circular pit dwellings and a large camp, 200 yds in diameter, near the track that leads from Tittle Row to Woolley and which is no longer discernible.

Two earthworks have been properly excavated and dated. The well-preserved Robin Hood's Arbour is situated on the Dutch Camp Road on Maidenhead Thicket. It has no association at all with the bandit of Sherwood Forest, nor is it of Roman origin as suggested by early Ordnance Survey maps. The earthwork is a ditched, rectilinear enclosure covering three-quarters of an acre with an entrance on the western side. The earliest mention of the earthwork was by Kerry in 1861, who favoured a Roman origin. In 1894 James Rutland and Henry Arrowsmith made what they termed an 'exhaustive investigation' and reported that little of interest or importance was found. A more scientific excavation took place in 1960, directed by Mrs Molly Cotton, and as a result of this we have a clearer picture of the purpose of the earthwork. The ditches, which were U-shaped, were 16ft wide and 3ft deep, just short of the solid chalk level. The loam from the ditch was used to make an inner bank forming an enclosure, but with no signs of a wooden palisade.

An entrance on the west side was found to be a simple gap with a causeway 10ft wide. A roughly cobbled trackway of flint and chalk passed through the entrance. The interior of the enclosure showed no signs of structures of any type but was interpreted as a paved stockyard. A small fire-hole was the only feature found which may have belonged to a night watchman guarding stock. The final conclusion was that

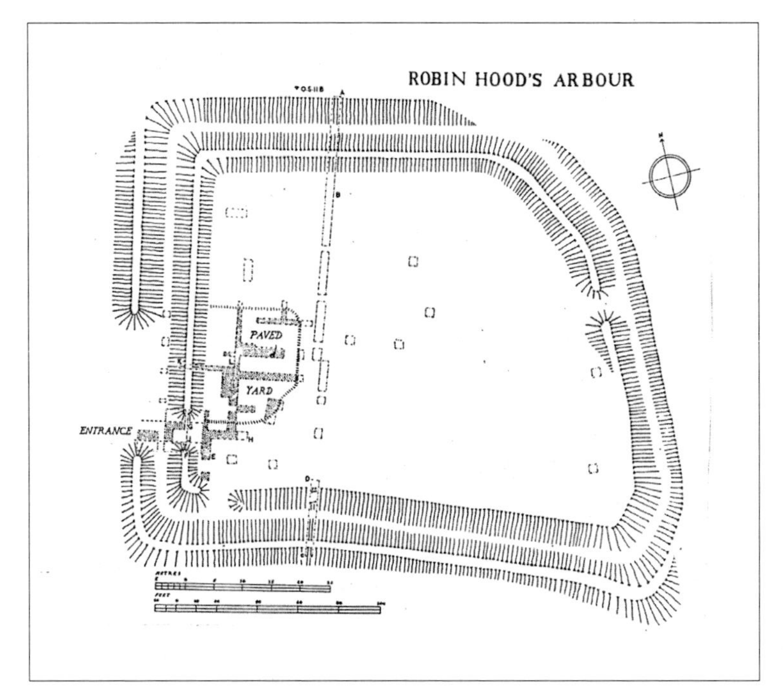

Plan of Robin Hood's Arbour, Maidenhead Thicket.

Excavation at Robin Hood's Arbour.

of an animal enclosure. Animal bones representing remains of meals were excavated, together with 130 pieces of Belgic pottery. A tentative date betwwen AD 1 and AD 43 was assigned to the earthwork. Another linear feature near Thicket Corner was excavated in 1982 prior to the construction of the new road, and this is thought to be a boundary ditch of roughly the same date.

The origins of the Thicket lay in the establishment of the Royal Forest of Windsor, of which it was an integral part. In the twelfth century the Norman Kings, sited at Windsor, ordered that East Berkshire be made into a forest area. By 1225 the Seven Forest Hundreds had been set up and by 1260 one general court was formed to run the whole forest and to ensure uniform administration for an area with royal game and creatures of chase. By 1268 it is recorded in the Assize Rolls that a Roger de Fryht was appointed bailiff of the Seven Hundreds. By 1321 the rights of the common people to remove wood from the Thicket were properly recognised. In an inquisition held at Elynton (Maidenhead) in that year before the Constable of Windsor, it was stated that:

> All tenants of the manors of Cookham and Bray since time immemorial have their profits of all open spaces and groves in the said manors within the boundaries of the Forest of Windsor – to wit La Thickette and Bigfrythe. Tenants have housebote, haybote and fuel with common pasture for all animals.

The Crown left the day-to-day running of the forest areas to the various landholders. Each area appointed a woodward, an officer whose job was to look after the woodlands and function as a forester and gamekeeper. In 1500 a forest return states that there were nineteen woodwards in Windsor Forest, of which the following covered the areas of Maidenhead Thicket:

> Andrew Wynch covered Altwood for the Queen; William Mattynglee covered Littlewick Wood for the Abbot of Chertsey; Thomas Fennynge covered Thicket and Knight lo for Sir William Norrreys of Ockwells; Richard Warner covered Inwood and Bigfrith for the Queen; John Shephard covered Waltham for the Bishop of Winchester; John Penvery covered Heywood (Woodlands Park) for the Abbot of Waltham Cross; Robert Nores covered Hurley Wood for the Prior of Hurley and Thomas Clers covered Bisham Woods for the Prior of Bisham.

At the Dissolution in 1538, ownership of ecclesiastical holdings changed radically and they moved into private hands.

From the above it can be seen that the Thicket was once a much larger area, and this is borne out by the words of the antiquary Lelend who passed through Maidenhead in 1538. After leaving the town he stated that 'for two miles the road was narrow and woody; then came the Great Frith, a wood infested with robbers some five miles in extent'. This would indicate that the Thicket extended past Knowl Hill into Hurley and Wargrave parishes. The Frithe, as mentioned by Leland, is the earliest name given to the Thicket and simply means 'wood or wooded country'. In the Assize Rolls of 1284 the 'Thicket of Cokeham' is mentioned. In 1370 it is styled 'Le Thikket by Maydenhythe'. In a lease dated 1606, it is divided into two areas and quotes the Thicket as being 160 acres abutting on the south to a wood called Altwood and being south of the Henley Road. To the north of the Henley Road, it is known as the Nockett and extends for seventy acres to Piggines gate (Pinkneys). Nockett indicates an oak wood, and this is confirmed in 1609 by the use of the name Oaken Grove, which today lives on in the road of the same name.

The Thicket was reduced in size at the time of the enclosure, and in 1589 a Cookham man complained that this action was 'to the great undoing of the poorer sort' who were unable to get wood for their Christmas fire. In the Second World War, sixty-four acres of land were requisitioned and ploughed up, making the Thicket even smaller. The area was a haven for footpads and rogues for many centuries, and as early as 1255 the Henley Road was widened to combat the element of surprise. Robbery was particularly prevalent during the coaching era when travellers refused to cross the Thicket by night. Those travelling from the west were preferred, as those coming from the east had in most cases been robbed on Hounslow Heath! There is the story of how the Vicar of Hurley was regularly stopped when he visited Maidenhead Chapel, and was paid danger money for crossing the Thicket. Another recounts how an ostler at the Sun Inn, Maidenhead, held up coaches and then sympathised with his victims when he heard their story at the inn.

Of the 'gentlemen of the road', only William Hawkes – 'the flying highwayman' – is known with certainty to have worked the Thicket. He often dressed as a soldier, farmer or clergyman to fool his victims. Dick Turpin, who appears in many local place names, is not thought to have worked in this area, but at his trial in York for a crime committed in that area, he tried to establish an alibi by telling the jury that he was in Maidenhead at the time of the incident. The details of a hold-up were recorded in *Jacksons Oxford Journal* on 1 November 1755, where it was stated that:

> Last Tuesday, about twelve o'clock at noon, the Oxford Machine, in which were three gentlemen, was stopped by a single highwayman well mounted, with a black mask, in Maidenhead Thicket. Upon demanding their money, the passengers gave him about twelve guineas; he then demanded their watches, which two of the gentlemen delivered; but one of them desiring he would return the Seal, on which was his coat of arms, the highwayman observing that the watch was only a Pinchbeck, said it would be of little service to him, and returned it. He then made off into the Thicket. The same person attempted to stop the Abingdon machine near the same place, but there being several persons on the outside, and the coachman driving on very briskly, he let them pass.

In 1736 the situation was so bad that Thomas Darvill, the landlord of the Bear Inn, Maidenhead, was ordered to pay £20 for information leading to the arrest of any highwayman. With the practice of 'hue and cry' in Elizabethan times, whereby all in the hundred were liable to pay if criminals were not caught, the hundred of Beynhurst was exempt from collective liability for crimes committed on the Thicket.

At the time of the turnpikes a tollgate was situated by the milestone at Thicket Corner. This was demolished in 1864 when the Highways and Locomotives Act made turnpikes

MAIDENHEAD RACES.

TUESDAY, OCTOBER 10, 1775.

The LADIES PURSE of FIFTY POUNDS, *(the best of Three Four-Mile Heats) by any Horse, Mare or Gelding; Five Year Olds, to carry* 8st. 8lb. *Six Year Olds, to carry* 8st. 12lb. *and Aged Horses to carry* 9st. 3lb. *Those that have won one* 50l. *Plate this Year to carry* 3lb. *extraordinary, those that have won two* 50l. *Plates this Year, to carry* 5lb. *extraordinary, and those that have won three or more* 50l. *Plates this Year, to carry* 7lb. *extraordinary.*

	RIDER's NAMES and the Colours of their Dress.	1st Heat.	2d Heat.	3d Heat.
MR. Brown's br. horse, Crony, aged, (3 plates) 9st. 10lb.	William Barnes, Blue.	2	2	
Mr Rider's bay gelding, Casca, 6 years old, 8st. 12lb.	John Rider, Purple.	dis.		
Mr. Gwyn's ch. h. Culprit, 6 years old, (1 plate) 9st. 1lb.	Rider unknown.			
Mr. Jennings's bay horse, Nestor, aged, (2 plates) 9st. 8lb.	Thomas Garret, Orange.	4	dr.	
Mr. Dymock's bay horse, Zachary, aged, 9st. 3lb	J Reynard, Blue & White.	3	4	
Mr. Stacey's Fortune Hunter, 5 yrs. old, (2 plates) 8st. 13lb.	R. Lefenby, Bl & White.	6	dr.	
Capt. O'Kelly's b. h. Cassimus, 5 years old, (1 plate) 8st. 11lb.	Samuel Merrit, Red.	1	1	
		5	3	

WEDNESDAY, OCTOBER 11.

The TOWN PURSE of FIFTY POUNDS *(the best of three Two Mile Heats) by any Horse,* &c *not exceeding Four Years old last Grass; Colts to carry* 8st. 4lb. *and Fillies* 8st. 0lb. *and those that have won one* 50l. *Plate this Year to carry* 4lb. *extraordinary, those that have won two* 50l. *Plates this Year, to carry* 7lb. *extraordinary, and those that have won three or more* 50l. *Plates this Year, to carry* 10lb. *extraordinary.*

	RIDER's NAMES and the Colours of their Dress.	1st Heat.	2d Heat.	3d Heat.	
LORD Castlehaven's grey colt, Bosphorus, 8st. 4lb.	Edmund Allen, Red.	9	9	dis	
Mr. Adams's dun colt, Dunny (2 plates) 8st. 11lb.	William Bristow, Crimson.	8	8	1	1
Mr. Green's bay colt, Trimmer, 8st. 4lb.	John South, Yellow.	1	4	7	2
Mr. Duggins's bay colt, Lightfoot, (one plate) 8st. 8lb.	William Barnes, Striped.	2	10	6	
Mr. Tomb's bay colt Codrus, (one plate) 8st. 8lb.	Unknown.	7	1	8	3
Mr. Stephenson's's grey colt, (to be sold) 8st. 4lb.	Unknown.	3	3	dr.	
Mr. Rider's black colt, Ivory Black, 8st. 4lb.	John Taibot, Purple,	4	5	5	
Mr. Langbridge's grey colt, Burntcrust, 8st. 4lb.	John Brown, Yellow.	6	2	4	
Capt. Bertie's bay filley, Lady Catchet, 8st.	William Bloss, Yellow.	5	7	2	
Capt. O'Kelly's chesnut filley, Juno, 8st.	Giles Edwards, Red.	10	6	3	

THURSDAY, OCTOBER 12

The NOBLEMEN and GENTLEMENS SUBSCRIPTION PURSE of FIFTY POUNDS, *Give and take, free for any Horse, &c. Aged Horses of* 14 *Hands to carry* 8st. 7lb, *and to allow* 7lb. *for every Year under; and to carry* 3 lb. *extraordinary for every Plate they shall have won this Year.*

	RIDER's NAMES and the Colours of their Dress.	1st Heat.	2d Heat.	3d Heat.
MR. Tilbury's grey mare, Melissa, 6 years old, (1 plate) 13 hands, 3 inches, 1-half, 1-8th.—8st. 0lb. 6z.	Thomas Campbell, White.	3	2	
Mr. Watts's bay horse, Gudgeon, aged, 14h.—8st. 7lb.	William Griston, Crimson.	dr.		
*** To start at One o'Clock. [illegible]		1	1	
[illegible]		2	dr.	

Racecard for Maidenhead Races, 1775.

into main roads. The earliest reference to the Army using the Thicket was in 1638, when a letter from James Harrington to the Earl of Northumberland mentions a concentration of 3,000 troops encamped there. During the First World War, extensive trenching was carried out for Army manoeuvres, and in the Second World War, when Queen Wilhelmina of the Netherlands was staying at Stubbings House, her bodyguard lived in specially-erected huts situated each side of what is now known as Dutch Camp Road.

The Thicket has been connected with many sporting events, the best-known being the Meet of the Royal Buckhounds. The big event was on Easter Monday when they met at the Coach & Horses (now known as the Shire Horse), and gypsies with coconut shies turned the occasion into a fair. Many Maidonians turned out for the event. The last meeting of the Buckhounds took place on 11 January 1901. Adjoining the Thicket in the Altwood Road area was the Maidenhead Racecourse. This was certainly there by 1770, and was visited by George III and his family in 1787. The races were discontinued by around 1815.

The origin of the name 'Stubbings' is not known with certainty, but it has been suggested that it was 'the place of stubs' – indicating that a number of trees had been cut down to form a clearance in the Thicket. The earliest record seems to be when Stubbings House was erected in 1756, and a Mr Cambler, a councillor at law, lived in it. At this time there were no other buildings in the area. The house was purchased by Elisha Biscoe, who lived there until 1790, when it passed to Guy Carlton, the first

Stubbings Church.

Baron of Dorchester. The baron had distinguished himself by being the Quarter Master General in 1759 under General Wolfe at Quebec. In 1775 he was appointed Governor of Quebec and Governor General of Canada. With his wife, Lady Maria, he had nine sons and two daughters. He died in Stubbings House in 1808. In the same year the house was acquired by Colonel Brotherton of the Lancers, and by 1830 had been purchased by Henry Skrine of Warleigh Manor, near Bath, for £12,000. Mr Skrine became lord of the manor of Cookham in 1849 when he purchased the property from Anne Vansittart of Bisham.

Mr Skrine, who had developed his fortune through tea in India or Ceylon, was responsible for the settlement at Stubbings, and provided land for the church, school, vicarage and 'Camley Cottage' where John Penny, parish clerk and sexton, lived from 1861 to 1921. Henry Skrine died in 1853 and his widow in 1866, and their tomb is inside the church. After the Skrine dynasty, the house was bought by Lawrence Wethered, who had an interest in the Marlow Brewery, and was related to one of the best-known vicars of Hurley. By 1897 the house was in the possession of the Crocker family and then the Smiths. Another notable owner was the scientist Sir Thomas Merton, who was an expert on light refraction. Stubbings House was the hideout of Queen Wilhelmina of the Netherlands during the Second World War, as described above. In 1976 it became the home of Dudley Good and his family.

The church at Stubbings is over 150 years old, having been consecrated on the 16 April 1850 by the Reverend Samuel Wilberforce, Bishop of Oxford. The foundation stone had been laid on 1 May 1849, and as 1 May was the festival day of St Philip and St James, the building was dedicated to St James the Less.

The land on which the church was built was purchased and donated by Henry Duncan Skrine, who was living at Stubbings House. The architect was Richard Cromwell Carpenter who also designed Cookham Dean Church and its twin churches in Australia and Tasmania. The builder was Richard Silver of Tittle Row, who donated the small, round west window. The side aisle was added in 1854 and the choir vestry as late as 1962, from a design by Gareth Slater. Materials for the building of the vestry came from All Saints, Braywood, which was demolished in that year. Some corbels from this latter church can be seen on the exterior walls.

The church was first served by the Reverend Edward Thring and Reverend G.N. Hodson, incumbent of Cookham Dean. Mr Skrine then built a vicarage and appointed his son, Wadham Huntley Skrine, as the first vicar in November, 1852. In 1874 the parish of Stubbings was created from parts of Cookham and Bisham parishes. In 1880 the first vicar died, and twenty years later Mr Skrine's eldest son, Herbert Henry, was instituted as the fourth incumbent. There is some interesting stained glass and brasses in the building. The extensive churchyard contains the graves of the Skrine family and of Lord and Lady Docker who lived in the parish. The Soltau Church Centre was dedicated by the Bishop of Reading in May 1997. It was funded partly by the sale of the old school and schoolhouse across the road.

Chapter Seven

Hurley

In 1988 England celebrated the tercentenary of the Glorious Revolution – the thankfully bloodless affair which secured Anglican rule in the Church and provided us with the democratic Parliamentary system that we know today. When William of Orange marched from Torbay to London in November of that year to claim the throne from James II, there was a skirmish at Maidenhead Bridge. But before that a local hero John, Lord Lovelace, had secretly plotted the downfall of James in the crypt of Ladye Place, a mansion built on the monastic remains of the Benedictine priory at Hurley.

When James II was proclaimed King on 11 February 1685, the corporation were pleased to celebrate the event. The Bridgemaster's Accounts tell us that £11 was spent on a dinner at the Greyhound Inn with 'bread, beer and wine, and two barrels and a kilderkin of beer set in the street' for the townsmen at a further cost of £2. When the coronation took place on 23 April, another £3 was spent on 'beer for the market'. But these celebrations were short-lived as they were soon to discover that the King was an ardent Catholic, and had plans to make England a mere satellite of France. James' grand design was a human rights campaign to establish religious tolerances for all Non-Conformists and free his fellow Catholics from the penal restrictions which had made them a harassed minority. To this end, he swept away all the century-old laws and, without approval of Parliament, granted full civil rights to all Catholics for the first time since the reign of Elizabeth I. Catholic men replaced Army officers, court officials and the Privy Council. Around the country, James appointed and dismissed town officials at will, and treated the Church of England in a malicious manner. The last straw was when the King issued his Declaration of Indulgence for all non-Anglicans, and imprisoned seven bishops who objected.

The eyes of England turned to the Hague and Prince William of Orange. In the Dutch Republic the accession of James II had had one important consequence. His eldest daughter, Mary, had become direct heir to the English throne, and had married her cousin William, who was also Protestant. Mary had promised William that if she ever came to the throne that they would rule together. This was reassuring to the English who knew that the succession was in safe Protestant hands.

Hurley Church and refectory.

But James delivered one final blow in late 1667 when his Queen, Mary Beatrice, after several miscarriages, suddenly became pregnant. If the child was a boy he knew that the Catholic succession would be secure, and if a girl, he had plans for the House of Commons to rubberstamp any pro-Catholic measures he chose to put forward. As it occurred, the Queen gave birth to a baby boy, who became the subject of a smear campaign where it was suggested that he had been smuggled into the delivery room in a warming pan. There was only one solution to this crisis, and that was to invite William of Orange to invade England and occupy the throne, and seven powerful men plotted to do just this. One key man who helped to trigger off this revolution was John, Lord Lovelace of Ladye Place, one of a long line of Lovelaces concerned with the administration of Berkshire.

Richard Lovelace had been High Sheriff and Lord Lieutenant of the county, as well as Deputy Constable at Windsor Castle. His son, Sir Richard, the first baron, had been Keeper of the Rolls, High Sheriff and the first named High Steward of Maidenhead in 1623. The second baron, John, who succeeded to the title in 1634, was the father of the third baron, John, the revolutionary in our story.

Both Johns were present at Maidenhead on 17 November 1662 when the warden, Edward White, and two burgesses, Thomas Hughes and Jonathan Attwater, were removed from the corporation for their Catholic convictions. John was born in 1641 and at the age of twenty became the MP for Berkshire. The following year he married Martha Pye of Bredenham Manor, High Wycombe, who was endowed by her father with the Hurley Manor estate comprising the parish of Hurley, Littlewick Green, Knowl Hill and eight working farms.

In the House of Commons, John was an opponent of the chimney tax, not surprising perhaps as he had thirty chimneys of his own. He moved upstairs to the

The monks' tithe barn and dovecoat at Hurley.

Lords on the death of his father in 1670, at which time he took over the title of baron and moved into Ladye Place.

He was distinguished, wrote Macauley, 'by his taste, by his magnificence, and by the audacious and intemporate vehemence of his Whiggism'. As a leading and fearless activist against Catholicism or 'Popery,' as it was indelicately called, he had been arrested six times for his convictions and was a natural choice to spearhead the Revolution that was about to take place.

In June 1688, Lord Lovelace held parties at Ladye Place under the cover of which he called secret meetings in the crypt. It was here, in the vaulted cellar which once echoed with the footsteps of Benedictine monks, that the plan to support William when he landed was adopted by the leading Thames Valley gentry. A brick-lined main sewer, which linked the crypt with the Thames, afforded an escape route for the revolutionaries if required. There was a similar tunnel connecting Ladye Place with Ye Olde Bell, a former monastic hostelry in the village where some of the plotters stayed overnight.

On 30 June the letter requesting William to invade was smuggled into Holland by Admiral Herbert, disguised as an ordinary seaman. The Prince of Orange accepted the invitation and in September Lovelace secretly slipped across the channel to visit William and assure the Prince of his support in the strategically important Thames Valley, securing the river highway between Oxford and Windsor.

Accordingly the 'Protestant Armada' of fifty warships set sail from Holland with William in command, and landed at Brixham on 5 November 1688. Ironically, on the same date in 1605, the boot had been on the other foot, when Guy Fawkes and the conspirators had attempted to blow up Parliament in the Catholic cause.

With his considerable army, William began his long march to London to claim the throne. On 10 November, Lovelace rode west from Hurley with seventy men to add his support. Alongside him was Bulstrode Whitelocke of Phyllis Court, Henley, who was killed in a skirmish with the Duke of Beaufort at Cirencester. At the same time Lovelace was captured and imprisoned at Gloucester Castle, but was released after William threatened to burn down the duke's mansion at Badminton. William entered Berkshire on 6 December and slept at Littlecote House. On 10 May he was in Newbury, in Wallingford the next day and by 12 December he had entered Henley. He was welcomed by a delegation which included Daniel Defoe, and spent the night either with the Whitelockes at Phyllis Court or with Colonel Freeman at Fawley Court. On 14 December he left Henley for Windsor, passing by Ladye Place on the way.

At Maidenhead Bridge he met opposition, firstly from Irish mercenaries hired by King James and secondly from two battalions of the Scotch Guards, who the diarist Samuel Pepys records as 'being quartered at Maidenhead under the command of Lieutenant-General Douglas'. Fortunately there was no bloodshed as the Guards decided to join the Prince, and the 'Mounted Micks' disappeared smartly over Maidenhead Bridge when they heard the Dutch drummers strike up a march. They may well have had to swim for it if James had kept his promise and destroyed the bridge as recorded in a letter from Thomas Oldfield, a Bristol solicitor to Sir John Newton. When William arrived in Abingdon he heard the news that James had fled the country with the Queen Mary and the baby Prince, to spend the rest of their life in exile in France.

After four days at Windsor Castle, during which time his troops were moved out of the Great Park because too many of the royal deer were being barbecued, William marched on to London. In spring 1689, after agreeing to a Declaration of Rights which was read to them, William and Mary were crowned King and Queen of England. In recognition of his services, King William appointed Lord Lovelace as Captain of the Gentlemen Pensioners, and in September 1690, after the Battle of the Boyne, visited him at Ladye Place. To celebrate the first anniversary of the revolution, Lovelace organised a race meeting on 21 October 1689 which he advertised in the *London Gazette* as follows:

> This is to give notice that my Lord Lovelace's Plate is to be run for on Cliveden Heath or Common and the Dinner to be held in The Bear at Maidenhead, there being no room at Hurley for the Gentlemen and their horses.

John, Lord Lovelace, died on 21 September 1693 at Ladye Place and was placed in the family vault in Hurley Church, where he lies with sixteen other Lovelaces. No one erected a memorial to his name or fame, perhaps because there was no money to pay for one…

He left £20,000 in debts, which were met from the sale of Ladye Place to Mrs Williams, sister of the Bishop of Rochester, who had won the money in a lottery. The Williams family later sold the mansion to Admiral Kempenfeldt who went down aboard the *Royal George* at Spithead. Ladye Place was eventually demolished in 1838. However the crypt, haunted by shrouded monks and echoes of the Glorious Revolution, remains to remind us of the plot which ended seventy years of struggle between the King and Parliament.

View of Ladye Place, Hurley, 1832.

Most of the later manor lords lived in Hall Place, Burchetts Green, built by William East in 1728. This mansion was sold by Lady Clayton East in 1948 and is now the East Berks College of Agriculture.

The Clayton Easts were lords of the manor for more than 130 years. Many of the family died in tragic circumstances, including Sir Robert, who was struck down with a mysterious illness on the lawn at Hall Place and died almost immediately at the age of twenty-four. This was in 1932, only four months after he had taken part in an expedition to find the legendary oasis of Zerzura near the Egyptian border. His young widow was killed in an air crash a year later, and it was rumoured locally that the couple had died of the curse of the Pharoahs, which had apparently been inflicted on those who had opened the tomb of Tutankhamun ten years earlier.

One of the most interesting stories was that discovered in a document stored in the Public Record Office. It concerned Lord Lovelace, the second Baron of Hurley, who lived in Ladye Place. On 9 October 1666 at the Hurley Manor court he examined one Edward Taylor, a boy of ten years, who provided an eye witness account of how his father and uncle started the Great Fire of London one month before by throwing fire balls through the window of the King's baker's shop in Pudding Lane. These men were clearly terrorists and were responsible for a blaze which lasted for four days and destroyed St Paul's, eighty-seven parish churches, the Guildhall, and 13,000 houses. Lord Lovelace produced the following report of the court proceedings:

> The examined saith he is the son of Joseph Taylor living in York Street, Covent Garden, who was employed by Joseph Taylor, a Dutchman and baker there, and is a brother to the Examined's father. And that this Examined was with his father and his uncle Joseph Taylor

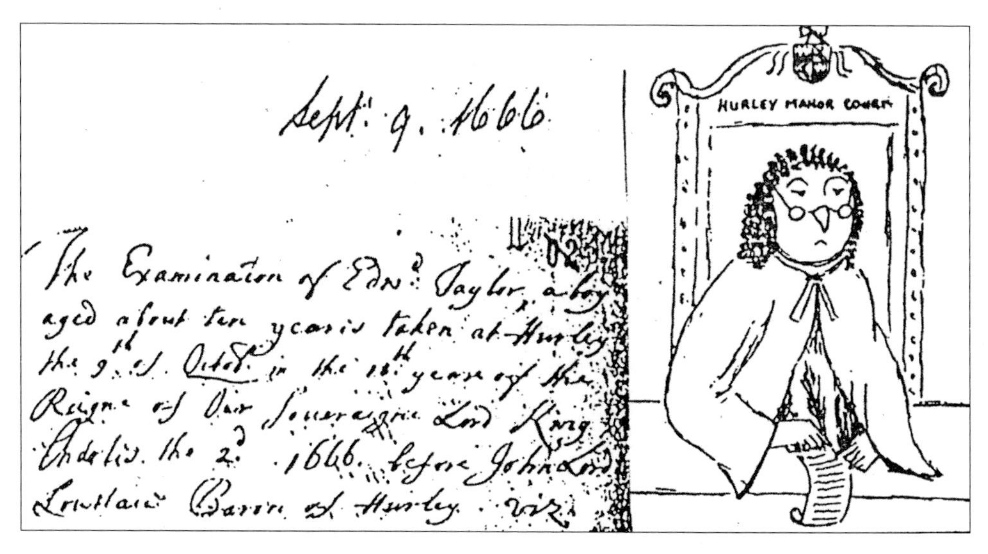
Sept: 9. 1666

The Examination of Edw. Taylor a boy aged about ten years taken at Hurley the 9th of Octob. in the 18th year of the Reign of Our Sovereign Lord King Charles the 2d 1666 before John Lord Lovelace Baron of Hurley viz.

Lord Lovelace at the trial of Edward Taylor, 1666.

> in Pudding Lane near London Bridge upon Saturday night the second day of September where they found a glass window open. Presently after they took two fire balls made of gunpowder and brimstone and fired them and then did fling them into ye said window and fired the house, but whose it was the examined knows not. And this was the first beginning of the firing of London. And from Pudding Lane this examined's father and uncle with two or three others went into Thames Street and Fleet Street and cast into several houses the like balls ready fired and after that they went to the old Exchange and did the like, and so went on doing such mischiefs two or three nights and days one after another. And that there were divers Frenchmen, Dutchmen, women and boys did go about the City with fire balls for that purpose. And that his uncle hired his father and gave him seven pounds to undertake this firing.

The boy's mother, Mary Swan, is believed to have been a prostitute, and went around in a black silken suit and cloak. There is no record as to whether the boy was convicted of a crime, but his evidence would undoubtedly have led to the conviction of his father and uncle if they could have been located.

The reason as to why such an important case should have been heard in Hurley Manor court is not recorded, but the likelihood is that the courts in London had been destroyed in the fire. Furthermore, the Great Plague of 1665 was still raging in the city and justices would want to give this hazard a wide berth. A similar situation occurred when Sir Walter Raleigh's trial was held at the Greyhound Inn at Maidenhead.

Chapter 8

Taplow

The ancient manor of Taplow has its origins in the Anglo-Saxon period, and for the past 1,000 years has had an impressive list of manor lords, mostly titled and at the very least candidates for the 'Who's Who?'. When one considers where these eminent men might have lived, the names Cliveden and Taplow Court immediately spring to mind, and this is true in many cases. However, there is a third residence which may have a claim to being the original manor house of Taplow. This is Amerden Bank, situated on the Buckinghamshire bank of the Thames close to Bray Lock. Taplow is an elongated parish of 1,762 acres, of which 473 are arable, 616 are grass and 322 woodland. The whole parish is bordered on the west by the river and divided into north and south by the Bath Road.

On the high ground to the north is Taplow Heath, with the house and grounds of Cliveden. Southwards is Taplow Court, to the east of which lies the present village. The ground then descends sharply to the level of the flood plain. To the south of the Bath Road the land stretches across arable land to Amerden and the Thames. This whole area is largely undeveloped and has seen little change in the last 1,000 years. This is probably why, when one walks the land, there is the feeling of crossing a medieval landscape.

The settlement of Taplow seems to have taken its name from the Saxon Taeppa Hloew, which translates as the 'mound of Taeppa'. The said Taeppa seems to have been a Saxon chieftain of some importance who lived during the seventh century, and the mound that is his burial tumulus still stands to a height of 15ft on the public ground adjacent to Taplow Court. This enormous mound was excavated in 1884 by James Rutland, a Taplow antiquary, and found to contain an Anglo-Saxon treasure second only to Sutton Hoo.

The grave goods, which included swords, spears, knives, bowls, glasses, drinking horns and numerous gold jewellery, are prominently displayed in the British Museum, and reflect the importance of the deceased, whose skeleton was found to be adorned with gold braid. The date for this pagan burial is given as AD 625.

Following in St Augustine's footsteps, Birinus, a bishop from Rome, established himself at Dorchester-on-Thames in AD 635 and preached Christianity to the West Saxons.

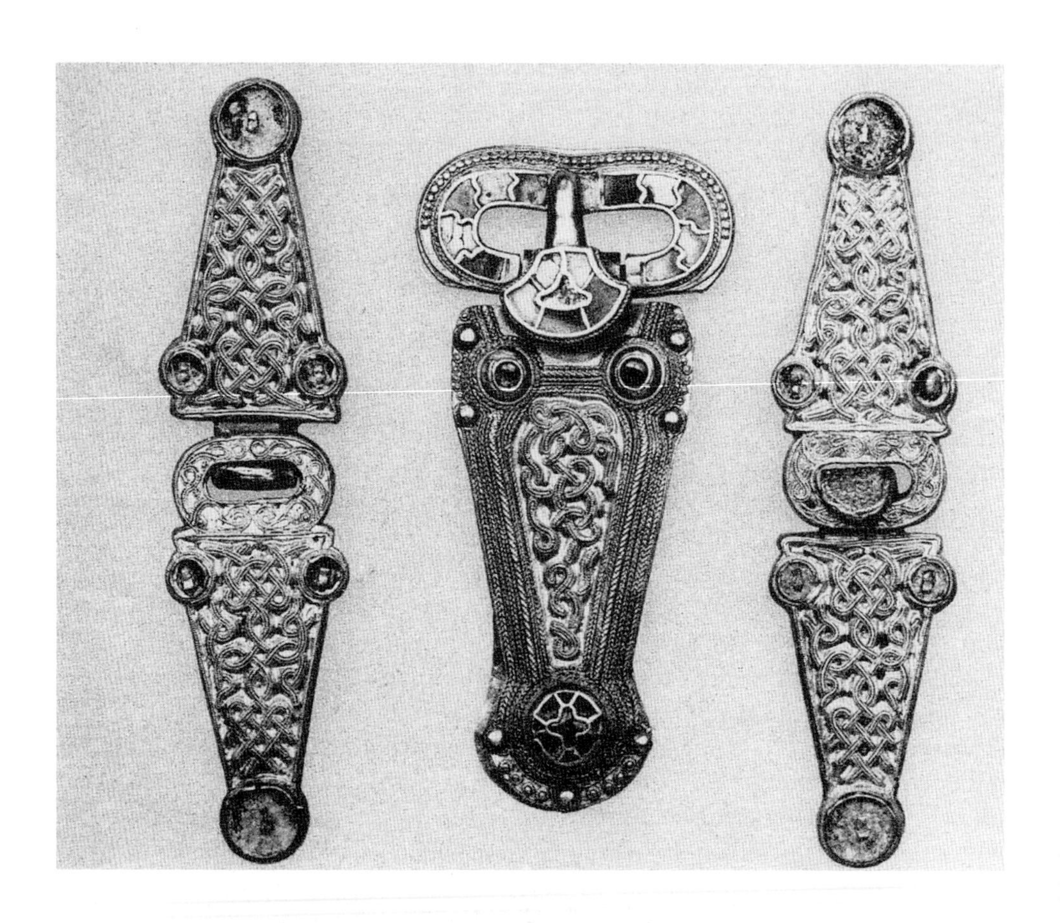

Finds from the Saxon barrow at Taplow, excavated in 1884.

The Saxon barrow and one of the Orkney tombs.

A pool to the south of the burial mound, known as the Bapsey Pond, is said by local legend to be the place where the inhabitants of Taplow were first baptised by Saint Birinus. In AD 871, when the Danes were in Reading, the Saxon lord of Taplow is recorded as Astig. In 1066, just prior to the Norman Conquest, the *Domesday Book* states that the manor was held by Asgot, a man of King Harold.

After the Conquest the land was taken from Asgot and given by King William to his brother Odo, Bishop of Bayeux, who in turn leased it to Roger. At Domesday it paid tax for eight hides and one virgate (about 1,000 acres), and had enough land for sixteen ploughs. There was a fishery in the Thames valued at 1,000 eels per annum, meadow for one plough and enough woodland to feed 700 pigs. The population was about ninety people and the value of the manor was £8. The location of the Norman village is a matter of conjecture. Land in front of Taplow Court, known anciently as Berry or Bury fields, and reflected in the name Berry Hill, may indicate the site of the former settlement and is close to the present village.

Certainly the earlier Church of St Nicholas was located nearby, with the Saxon tumulus as part of its churchyard. The old church was demolished in 1828 and some remains could still be seen in 1853. The present church was built in 1828, enlarged in 1865, and rebuilt in 1912 in the fourteenth-century style. Some relics of the old church have been preserved, the earliest being a twelfth-century marble base which points to the fact that it had been standing since Norman times.

But where were the Saxon and Norman manor houses located? To decide this it is necessary to trace the history of the three main residences – Taplow Court, Cliveden and Amerden, all of which have been associated with the lords of the manor.

By the twelfth century the original manor lands of Taplow had been separated by subinfeudation, forming the manors of Amerden and Cliveden. This began in 1197 when the then owner, William de Turville, leased the Amerden part to the Prior of Merton. The manor then passed to William Piscator, whose son Stephen inherited Amerden and Cliveden, but did homage for his lands in 1213 to Merton Priory. When he died, his sons became Geoffrey of Cliveden and William of Amerden and the manor was truly divided, with the priory maintaining the use of the Amerden section.

The descent of Taplow Manor as a whole is complicated due to the many leases issued over the years, but basically Merton Priory held the lands from 1197 until the Dissolution in 1533 when Thomas Manfield took them over. The Manfields leased portions of the land until 1635 when it passed to Thomas Hampson. In 1700 he sold it to George, Earl of Orkney, whose family held it until a land sale in 1852 when it was bought by Charles Pascoe Grenfell, who in turn passed it down to his son, William Henry, created Lord Desborough in 1905.

Of the three large houses, Cliveden can be eliminated as an early manor house. The mansion and its 300 acre park was originally built by George Villiers, Duke of Buckingham, in the seventeenth century and was visited by John Evelyn on 23 July 1679, who described the estate as 'that stupendous natural rock, wood and prospect – buildings of extraordinary expense, the cloisters, descents, gardens and avenue through the wood, august and stately; but the land all about wretchedly barren, and producing nothing but fern'.

Taplow Court and burial ground.

Cliveden is mentioned as an estate before the house was built. The Manfields owned it in 1669 when it was said to contain 'fifty acres of wood and a building called the Lodge'. By 1573 there were two lodges, old and new, and arable land comprising the park amounted to 160 acres. Common of pasture in Taplow Wood and Green Common was claimed in 1610 in right of the park. In the sixteenth century, the area appeared as Cliveden Park, alias Mansfield's (not to be confused with the Mansfield Park in the Jane Austin novel).

The house was added to and changed by the Earl of Orkney in the early eighteenth century, and occupied for some time by Frederick, Prince of Wales. The Orkneys held it until 1830 when it was sold to Sir George Warrender, after which it passed to the Duke of Sutherland before being bought by the Astor family in 1890. During its existence, the house was destroyed by fire in both 1795 and 1849. The present house was erected in 1851 and is now a hotel.

The site of Taplow Court is the most logical place for a manor house to be located. Situated at the top of Berry Hill and close to the present village, it stands at the centre of Saxon activity and adjacent to the site of the earlier church and its graveyard. The history of the building, however, is hazy – although we do know that the present court was built in 1855 by the Grenfell family.

A previous house on the spot was the residence of the Hampson family in the seventeenth century and is known to have been partly rebuilt by the Earl of Orkney a century later.

The earliest reference seems to be in 1610, when Sir Henry Guilford was granted a lease of the site of the manor house, which is recorded as having been burned down in 1616.

It is possible that this manor house was the residence of the Cliveden section of the manor of Taplow formed in the twelfth century.

This leaves the Amerden complex as the most likely site for the earliest manor house in Taplow, existing at Domesday and perhaps even before the Conquest. As previously mentioned, it was a religious house and a cell of Merton Priory from 1197 until the Dissolution. An earlier version of the name Amerden, spelt Amerton, suggests that it might have derived from 'A Merton Priory'.

At the time the priory took over the site, it was described as three virgates and two acres, and an assail with fishing in the Thames, which in modern terms is just over 100 acres in size. A clue to the possible pre-Conquest existence of Amerden comes from the Domesday entry for Taplow in 1086, where it is stated that a monk of Stigand, the ejected Archbishop of Canterbury, held one hide in Taplow Manor before 1066. One hide is about 120 acres, which may well equate with the land held by the priory, and the entry may also indicate previous use of the site by a religious house.

The present complex consists of Amerden Bank and Amerden Priory, the latter being the older with some thirteenth-century roof timbers. Another indication of early use is that both houses on the site are surrounded by three sides of a moat, with the river representing the fourth side. The history of Amerden Manor is well-documented, and by 1340 the Piscator family had taken the name Aumberdene (Amerden). In that year Richard de Aumberdene was prosecuted for fishing in the fishery of Queen Philippa in her manor at Bray and removing weirs and stakes there. His brother, Nicholas de Aumberdene, was buried in Taplow's old church in 1350, and a brass to his memory can still be seen in the present church.

Cliveden House, *c.* 1785.

During their tenancy in 1377, a Hameldon Lock was erected, probably in the position now occupied by Bray Lock. The toll was said to be exorbitant, and the lock was taken up in 1510. Another lock was removed in 1622 by order of the Commissioner of Sewers.

In 1410 Amerden became the property of Thomas Manfield, whose family held it until 1703 when it was sold to Budd Wase. By 1720 it was in the possession of George Hamilton, the Earl of Orkney. During the time that the Orkneys owned the property, they claimed the right to supplying horses and towing barges from Windsor to Boulters Lock.

Part of the Amerden complex was then known as Moat Farm, and tenant farmers were mentioned as Lucas in 1771 and Aidridge in 1789. In the Taplow land sale of 1852, Amerden was bought by Charles Whitlaw, who married and brought his wife to the house in 1874.

Selina Whitlaw was an obsessive carver and spent eight hours per day for five years carving the staircase panels in the house. Her 'nursery rhyme' frieze started in the hallway, continued through two rooms and then onto the gables outside. She lived in the house as a widow until 1934, after which it was empty for a few years. During the Second World War it was used by the Westminster Health Authority as a home for evacuee babies. Later, it was a repository for a London firm.

Cyril de Lara Bell bought Amerden and lived in it for ten years and then, in 1959, it was purchased by Michael Browne. Mr Browne gave the building a complete overhaul, renewed the roof and removed five chimneys. During his renovations, he turned the old Merton Priory Chapel into a kitchen and the assembly hall into a dining room. During its chequered history, Amerden has also been a hotel and a doss house for bargees.

Like all old houses it has its resident ghosts, consisting of a coach full of people who, while travelling from London, lost control of their horses and drove into the river. There were no survivors. Or perhaps this was just the imagination of a drunken bargee as he walked the towpath at dusk?

Aviators

Benton and Allen, the early aviation pioneers from Maidenhead invented the biplane that was to be seen circling over Pinkneys Green, where Benton lived in a small cottage. Meanwhile, over the bridge at Taplow, another boffin was assembling a flying machine based on the principles of the helicopter. Helicopters were among the earliest of designs. The oldest dated back to 1490, when Leonardo da Vinci, the Florentine artist, designed a model. Had he had a source of propulsion his invention probably would have worked. At least he would have stood a better chance than the contemporary medieval tower jumpers who fell to their deaths with monotonous regularity.

The expert from Taplow was G.L.O. Davidson, originally from Aberdeen, who had taken residence at Amerden Bank. In a large shed in the back garden he had designed and assembled what be termed a 'gyrocopter', which resembled a biplane with helicopter rotors sandwiched between the wings. This flying machine worked on the principle of vertical take-off, with wings to stabilise horizontal flight. The whole contraption weighed seven tons, which was no light weight to lift off the ground. The rotor blades were powered by two 50hp engines. Davidson employed twelve engineers and draughtsmen while building the machine, which when completed cost £10,000. Considerable interest was shown by admirals and high-ranking officials who visited the site.

One distinguished visitor was Sir Edward Elgar, who lived just across the river in his house near Monkey Island Hotel. Another was the novelist H.G. Wells, who often dined there. By the nature of his writings, he was always interested in things to come.

There appears to be no record as to whether the invention ever got off the ground, but certainly the concept of the gyrocopter seems to have faded into obscurity.

Maidenhead & Taplow Field Club

Nowadays, local history can be studied by people from all walks of life, providing they obtain the minimum of guidance. Courses on the subject are available through the WEA (the Workers Education Association) or other extra-mural centres, and a wider knowledge can be obtained by joining a local group, such as the Maidenhead Archaeological & Historical Society.

However, things were not quite the same in the nineteenth century. On 18 September 1883, the Maidenhead & Taplow Field Club was formed. It was considered that archaeology and history were not pursuits suitable for the cloth-capped worker, and this was emphasised by 'Our Looker On' in the *Advertiser* when he wrote:

> Mr Pickwick conceived the great idea of founding a brotherhood of antiquarians, and his project was so rapturously received by his confreres, that there has been an openly professed regard among a certain class of intelligent people for such pursuit and diversions as are comprehended in the programme of a field club.

Quite clearly, membership of the Field Club was aimed at local gentry and middle-class Maidonians, when at an inaugural meeting in the council chamber under the presidency of the Mayor, the annual subscriptions were set at 10*s* per annum for gentlemen and 2*s* and 6*d* for ladies. For the average male worker, this represented at least five weeks' wages.

Be that as it may, the membership read like a 'Who's Who' in Maidenhead, and attracted such local antiquaries as Stephen Darby, A.H. Cocks, J. Wesley Walker, Colonel C.P. Serocold and Alderman Silver. Other well-known members included E.J. Shrewsbery, designer of the Art College and the Jubilee Clock Tower, and F.O. Baylis with his *Advertiser* connections.

The formation of the club followed a trend set by the Wiltshire Antiquarian Society for the study of our ancient ancestors. The objectives set were to collect and publish information on the antiquities of the Maidenhead neighbourhood and the Thames Valley, to visit and inspect objects of archaeological interest and to encourage scientific research.

The proposed excursions of the club were described by the *Advertiser* in the following flowery terms:

> There may be little excursions hither and thither, with opportunities for semi-scientific flirtations, or errant gossips in sylvan spots about lichens and fungi, or meanderings in ivy clad ruins, with panoramic peeps across vale and plain, and little stimulating discoveries of ancient latch keys and rust eaten wine taps, or perchance, the thrilling incident of a Roman stirrup iron chipped out of an ancient doorstep.

However one views this advance publicity, it must have proved irresistible to the Victorians as fifty-five people applied for immediate membership, and in the years to follow this increased considerably. One of the major attractions was undoubtedly the picnics held at ancient monuments – with hampers full of goodies provided by the ladies.

The Field Club was in existence from 1883 to 1891, during which time it produced a journal outlining its activities. Credit for this must go to the honorary secretary, James Rutland, who was the mainstay of the group, and himself a very active archaeologist. He carried out fieldwork on the Taplow Saxon Barrow, Robin Hood's Arbour and the earthwork at Spencers Farm. He also excavated Castle Hill Roman Villa in five days, in a somewhat unscientific manner.

Today we owe a lot to these antiquaries who provided extensive notes on the history of Maidenhead and its neighbour-hood. After the demise of the club in 1891, researchers had to rely on reports in the *Advertiser* or by private individuals until the formation of Maidenhead Archaeological Society in 1961, when the history of Maidenhead once more became documented.

Chapter Nine

The Hundred of Desborough

The most southerly of the Buckingham hundreds is that of Desborough, from which Lord Desborough took his name, even though his residence at Taplow Court was in Burnham hundred. The area covered by the hundred of Desborough was perhaps larger than most and extended from well above High Wycombe in the southern Chilterns to the Thames boundary, encompassing the settlement of Bourne End, Wooburn and Marlow.

Despite its large area, this hundred seems to have been sparsely populated in ancient times, with the usual prehistoric settlement along the banks of the Thames. During the Roman period, the economy of the area seems to have been based on sheep farming, with an estate administered from the wealthy and extensive Roman villa excavated on the Rye at High Wycombe.

An early black and white mosaic discovered in the building indicates the early prosperity of the owners, and a series of lead coffins found in Blind Lane, Bourne End, may well be their place of burial. Evidence of later sheep farming comes from local place names like Sheepridge, Woolmans Wood and Sheepcote Wood, and the fact that Great Marlow had a wool fair from the seventh to nineteenth centuries.

Bourne End, now a thriving settlement, seems to have been an isolated area until the railway came in 1857. Although the place name Burnend was used in 1222, this merely indicated a place where the River Wye entered the Thames. Evidence of its isolation comes from the fact that gunpowder was manufactured on the site of Jackson's Mill between 1665 and 1715.

Another indication of the lack of habitation comes from an excavation in 1905, when numerous skeletons of Anglo-Saxon warriors, together with their weapons, were discovered between Bourne End station and Jackson's Mill at Egham's Green. The names Bone End and Cores (corpse) End on early maps may delineate the extent of such a cemetery which could be associated with the Burghal Hideage fort known to have been built by King Alfred on Sashes Island by AD 882. The name Egham in Saxon means island settlement, albeit to provide accommodation for the dead.

The *Domesday Book* indicates that the manor of Wooburn, which included Bourne End and Loudwater, was an extensive settlement situated on the Wye Combe, an early

The Railway Hotel and the station at Bourne End.

route through the Chilterns linking the Thames with the Upper Icknield Way. The manor was sited to take advantage of the River Wye which, from the earliest of times, has provided the water power for the numerous mills situated along its route. In 1086, eleven mills were recorded on the Wye, all presumably for the milling of flour.

Before the Conquest the manor of Wooburn belonged to the Earl Harold. Under Norman rule it was awarded to Remigius, the Bishop of Lincoln and a cousin of William I, who had provided ships and knights for the campaign. The bishop did not reside there but sub-let the manor to the Norman knight Walter D'Eyncourt, whose manor house stood opposite Wooburn Church. The population of the manor was around 100, with woodland to support 200 pigs and a fishery valued at 300 eels annually. By 1223 this manor had become known as Wooburn D'Eyncourt, and a significant change took place in the manorial structure with the creation of Bishop's Wooburn, after Bishop Hugh had taken action against his tenant Oliver D'Eyncourt. This was in the form of a bishop's palace built beside the Wye and moated by diverting the river to form an island. The complex included a chapel and a prison below ground, known as the Little Ease. Many bishops were in residence there, the last being the Bishop of Holbeach in 1547, after which the religious establishment was dissolved. Henry Berghersh, who was bishop in 1334, is said to have given his name to the settlement of Berghers Hill.

In 1547, Catherine of Aragon lodged at the Bishops Palace, and is said to have introduced lace-making to the area – this became a cottage industry on an extensive scale. In her honour, lace-makers in the valley celebrated the feast of St Catherine on 25 November. In 1562 the palace was transferred to John Goodwin, Sheriff of Buckingham, and it took on the title of Goodwins Manor, after which it passed by marriage to Philip, Lord Wharton, and remained in his family for some time.

The palace and chapel were demolished in 1750 with the exception of one stable wing, and Wooburn House was built on the site by a Mr Bertie in 1769.

A second manor, held at Domesday by the Bishop and Walter D'Eyncourt, was situated in north Wooburn and known as Lede or Lude. The last remaining vestige of this manor is Lude Farm, two miles north of the M40. However, it owned three mills on the River Wye which belonged in 1250 to William de la Lude, one of which was called Ludewater Mill. This is obviously how the name Loudwater came into existence, the slight corruption probably arising from the noise of the mill race.

Between Loudwater and Wooburn Town, a manor known as Glory was held in 1235 by John de la Gloria. While this has now disappeared, the title is perpetuated in the mill of the same name. The centre of the manor of Wooburn was at Wooburn Town, which has now been eclipsed by the larger settlement of Wooburn Green. The D'Eyncourt mansion which stood directly opposite the front of the church has now been demolished. The Church of St Paul, which dates back to *c.* 1180, was rebuilt in 1360 and had the tower added in 1442 by John Goodwin. Between 1856 and 1869, the church suffered the usual Victorian restoration under the Reverend Ashley, who was also responsible for the building of two schools in Wooburn.

The town itself has some good examples of medieval buildings, including Boscabel, once the Royal Oak public house. Two black seventeenth-century wooden figures on the front of the building are said to represent the architect and builder of the church, but this suggestion cannot be substantiated. Other ancient buildings include the old vicarage and the Post Office. To the north of the church are the remains of the Royal Stag Brewery, started by Thomas Williams in 1830.

Throughout history, the mills on the River Wye have provided a source of employment for the inhabitants of Wooburn. In 1816, no fewer than thirty-seven mills were recorded on the river, the majority of which are now silent. The best-known of these was perhaps Jackson's Board Mill, which employed over 1,000 people during the twentieth century. Other mills that readers will remember are the Glory, Princes, Soho End and Claptons.

By the thirteenth century, many of the Domesday corn mills had been converted to fulling mills in connection with the thriving cloth trade at High Wycombe. The fulling process involved placing the loosely-woven fabric in a vat containing water and fuller's earth, and by a stamping action that shrank and matted the material to convert it to a felted broadcloth.

In 1600, the mills were converted for paper making and thirty-two were used for this purpose by 1816. By order of Elizabeth I, rags were collected from all over the world for the manufacture of paper, but a temporary halt was made to this process in 1636 when it was thought that filthy rags may have carried the plague. This particularly affected the workers of Wooburn, as they were situated within ten miles of a royal household.

The Royal Oak at Wooburn in 1909. The building is now the house named 'Boscabel'.

The remains of Soho Mill on the River Wye at Wooburn.

After this setback, and problems with the initial supply of rags, the industry continued without hindrance until 1830 when Fourdrinier machines were introduced in the mills. Faced with unemployment and job losses, an angry mob of 1,000 men swept through the valley, smashing machinery at five of the mills. A total of 126 rioters were convicted and the ringleaders, John Sawney and Thomas Blizzard, narrowly missed a death sentence and were transported to Botany Bay, Australia.

For more than 1,000 years, the River Wye between Wycombe and Bourne End has been used as a source of power for the numerous fulling mills and those manufacturing paper and flour. When excise numbers were introduced in 1816 there were no fewer than thirty-one mills in operation, providing work for a large number of people. During the 1960s, Jackson's Mill supported 1,100 employees. But few will know of the explosives industry which used the same site in the seventeenth century. By piecing together new evidence unearthed in the Public Record Office, we now have a reasonably clear picture of the period when gunpowder was manufactured at Bourne End. Because of the nature of the industry and the frequency of explosions, it was necessary for such activities to take place in an isolated area, and this fits with the fact that virtually no buildings in the immediate vicinity predate 1700.

In 1222 the area known as Burn End, indicating the place where the River Wye ran into the Thames, was land belonging to the manor of Wooburn. It was well into the nineteenth century before it had the status of a settlement.

Aerial view of Jackson's Board Mill, once the site of a gunpowder mill.

Explosions were common in the early days of gunpowder manufacture, when one small spark could cause the devastation of a whole site, with a great loss of life. Wages were high because of the risk factor, but all too often a widow was left to bring up a family with no compensation for the death of her husband. Sites were large and spread out, as apart from the water-powered mills, there was a need for buildings to store the barrels of powder and the necessary ingredients of saltpetre, sulphur and charcoal.

At Bourne End a four-acre field shown on the Du Pre estate map of 1813 as Powder Mill Close probably accommodated these buildings. Manufacture of powder at Wooburn took place between the years 1665 and 1705 on land belonging to the Wharton family, who owned the manors of Bishops Wooburn and Wooburn D'Eyncourt at this time.

The Wharton dynasty at Wooburn began in 1658 when Philip, Lord Wharton, moved into the moated Wooburn House. The family continued to live here until 1731, when the manor was sold.

The mills were erected in 1665 by James Lloyd, a gunpowder manufacturer from Wandsworth, and it is recorded that he received £200 compensation 'for losses in erecting mills at Wooburn during the Second Dutch War [1665-71] only to find that they were not employed full time'. Gunpowder was much in demand at this time, not least of all because the Dutch fleet had sailed up the Medway and attacked Chatham in 1667.

However, manufacture was mainly confined to rural districts because of the disastrous effects on London of the plague in 1665 and the Great Fire of 1666.

By March 1673, the lease of Wooburn Mills was in the hands of Robert Richardson, who also had mills on Hounslow Heath. On his death, he left the mills to Sir Polycarpus Wharton. Sir Polycarpus, although not one of the Wooburn Whartons, was nevertheless related. He was the eldest son of Sir George Wharton, who was treasurer and paymaster to the office of the Royal Ordnance until his death in 1681.

Sir Polycarpus first supplied powder to the government in 1673 and was directed to take out a twenty-one year lease on Chilworth Mills, Surrey, in 1677, from which he was expected to produce 800 tons per year. His involvement with Wooburn probably began in 1680 when he successfully demonstrated some very strong powder before Charles II, who was a regular visitor to Wooburn House and godfather to some of the Whartons.

The King encouraged him to erect mills and works near Windsor much differing from the common sort, which may have been the first edge-runner mills in England, operating with a vertical round millstone.

The Powder Ledger in the Public Record Office gives Sir Polycarpus Wharton as the owner of the mills in 1682, and an entry on 6 October for '1,950 barrels of powder to be made at Chilworth, Woburne and Susan.' These were all mills belonging to Wharton, Susan being mills at Sewardstone, Essex, which he held from 1694 to 1700.

Gunpowder manufacture ceased at Bourne End by 1705 when the site was taken over by Emmanuel Wright, probably as a paper mill. As for Sir Polycarpus, he took out a second contract with the government to supply 400 tons of powder per year for the period 1687-95. Unfortunately for him these contracts were not honoured and he accrued debts of £24,000. By 1719 he was languishing in a debtors prison, while at Bourne End the dark satanic mills had disappeared from the scene.

Devastation caused by a gunpowder mill explosion in 1850.

Hedsor

Hedsor lies on the north bank of the River Thames opposite Cookham and in many ways does not have the identity of a separate settlement. There is no record of a manor existing in the *Domesday Book*, and evidence suggests that at this time it was land belonging to the manor of Little Marlow. There is no recognisable village as such, and it is likely that it has always been more of an estate than a place of habitation.

The name in Anglo-Saxon is the same as the combined suffixes of Maidenhead and Windsor; that is Hed-sor, 'the wharf on the river bank.'

Hedsor Wharf is known to have been in existence in 1195 – possibly much earlier. Situated as it is on a Thames backwater facing Sashes Island, it was in use all through the medieval period for the shipment of timber and building materials along the river. It stayed in use until 1914 for the movement of bricks and tiles to London until the local brick fields were no longer productive and the industry died in the area. Until recent years, a sunken way for horse-drawn carts was visible from Tower Hill to the riverside.

The residence at Hedsor Wharf was built by Lord Boston in 1764. A previous house with a 'new wharf' was mentioned in 1573, when the land and fishery belonged to Richard and Joan Over, coincidentally ancestors of mine. Their name perpetuates in Over's Farm, to the north of the parish. The Overs conveyed the property to Roland Hynd, who had purchased the manor in 1573. His grave lies in the churchyard of St Nicholas.

In Roman times the Camlet Way, the road linking the two Roman capitals of St Albans and Silchester, crossed the Thames by Hedsor Wharf. In 1894, heavy wooden piles were excavated at the confluence of Blessing's Brook which may represent the bridge carrying this road onto Sashes Island. Evidence suggests that there may have been a Roman inland port situated at this point of the Thames.

The Burghal Hideage document gives details of a fort built by King Alfred on Sashes Island by AD 882. This was after the period of numerous Danish raids which almost continuously destroyed settlements along the river.

It is likely that the Anglo-Saxon burgh or fort was controlled from Wallingford, the county town of Berkshire and the site of a much larger fort. This, perhaps, explains why the manor of Hedsor appears in 1166 as being attached to the Honour of Wallingford. Lands belonging to this manor descended by marriage to firstly Robert D'Oilly, who held the manor of High Wycombe at Domesday, and then to Miles Crispin who had land at Little Marlow.

It would seem that the manor of Hedsor emerged in the twelfth century, the first reference being in 1166 when it was held by Geoffrey, son of Sofrid, whose son William of Hedsor took over in 1202. Ownership passed through numerous families until it was purchased in 1764 by the second Lord Boston, who built himself a mansion on the site of Hedsor Lodge in 1778, and the famous folly on Tower Hill which remains a landmark. This was erected in memory of George III, who stayed in the house.

Hedsor Lodge itself was built in 1862. East of the church is a red-brick residence erected in 1844 on the site of the old manor house of 1584. Some vestiges of this earlier building, designed by Roland Hyde, remain together with the flint and clunch walls which enclose the garden and contain a stone inscribed 'R.H. 1583'.

To the north of the parish is the farm of Lilyfee, which represents the thirteenth-century Deserted Medieval Village of Linlei. In 1431 it was appurtenant to the Honour of Wallingford and under the same ownership as Hedsor. References to a court at Lilyfee occur in 1422 and 1431. Remains of this settlement are now below ground-level, and no excavation has taken place.

The Church of St Nicholas at Hedsor is small and probably indicative of a small population. The first mention we have of this building is in 1218, when it was under the control of the prioress and nuns of Marlow. From early times it was served by chaplains appointed by the priory and remained so until the Dissolution in 1536. The valuation of the building at the Dissolution stated that it belonged to the monastery of Little Marlow, where Marjorie Vernon was abbess and incumbent. The priory was first granted land near the church by William of Hedsor, after he had previously offered it to Missenden Abbey. The chancel and nave of St Nicholas are of medieval date.

The Domesday entries for Marlow are particularly complicated. While the manor of Great Marlow was held by Queen Matilda, Little Marlow was divided into three separate territories. The most easterly of these stretched from Bourne End to Spade Oak and was held before 1066 by Queen Edith, relict of Edward the Confessor. In 1070 this land passed to Odo, Bishop of Bayeux, brother of William the Conqueror, who leased it to the thane Theowald. The latter also held 360 acres from the bishop in Hanachdene, which has been identified as Winchbottom in the north of the parish.

The church at Hedsor.

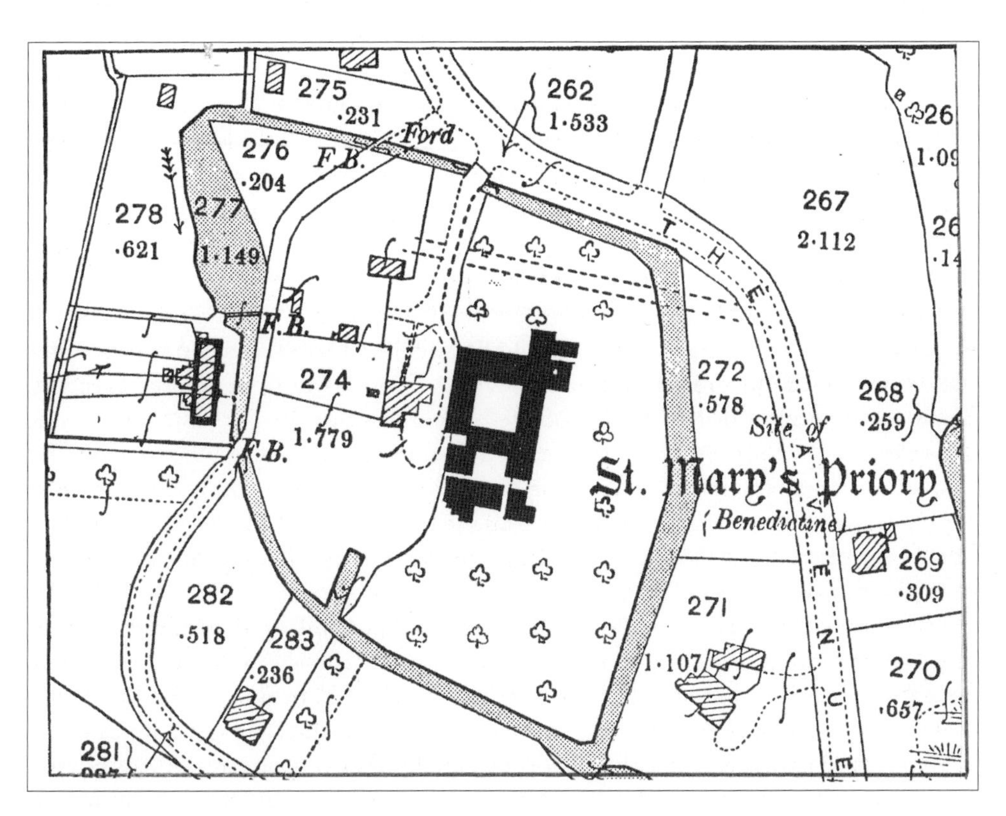

Plan of St Mary's Priory, Little Marlow.

Situated in this manor, on land now occupied by the Abbotsbrook estate, was the Little Marlow Priory or nunnery, which had control over the churches at Hedsor and Little Marlow. The priory was built by the Benedictines around 1215 on marshy ground near the river, with the streams forming a natural moat. Excavations carried out in 1902 by Vaughan Williams showed that the original church, cloister and reredorter were completed by 1220 and a transept added in 1250. In 1292, when Bishop Sutton of Lincoln dedicated the high altar on the feast of St Agatha, the choir was extended to the east. Bishop Dalderby dedicated a new kitchen and infirmary in 1311. Many of the buildings were still standing in 1719, but by 1813 it was reported that they had been dismantled and the stone used in neighbouring farms. After the Dissolution the land passed to Bisham Abbey.

In medieval times, Well End was known as the 'Fontibus de Merlaw' or the Marlow Fountain. Here a natural well existed which was associated with the priory and may have been a place of pilgrimage where votive offerings were made. It was known as Flaecca's Well and gave its name to an area called Flacwelle in 1227 – the Flackwell Heath of today.

Between Spade Oak and Little Marlow village were two early settlements with Norse names, which may have been temporary habitation sites of the Danes. The first of these was Coldmoorholm, the name of which suggests an island. The second was Westhorpe, translating as west hamlet. In the fourteenth century, this developed into the manor of Losemere. This manor was purchased in 1684 by James Chase, MP for Great Marlow, who built the present Westhorpe House in classical style.

Little Marlow still remains a backwater, and as such has retained its medieval layout with its church, manor house and farm. In 1086 it was held by Miles Crispin, who sub-let it to Ralph and Roger Danvers, sons of Roland De Anvers, who came over with William I. Later, the land was to become Danvers Manor, with the manor house adjacent to the church. Agnes Danvers is recorded as a patron of the priory in 1230.

The Church of St John the Baptist was first mentioned in 1219 and the south wall of the chapel and the chancel date to this period. The north aisle and tower were erected in the fourteenth century, and the south aisle added a century later. The Victorian restoration took place in 1866.

Chapter Ten

Binfield and Wargrave

The manor or parish of Binfield, which adjoins that of Waltham St Lawrence, has its own history. However its origins, like many other settlements, are lost in obscurity. There is no evidence to show that any form of village existed in Roman times when the first Bath Road, known as the Devil's Highway, crossed Berkshire four miles to the south on its way from Staines (Pontes) to the city of Calleva Atrebatum at Silchester.

Undoubtedly, the origins of the settlement are to be found in the late Anglo-Saxon period when manors were formed as agricultural units under the leadership of a feudal lord. At this time, the manor was called Beinfeld, a name which describes 'the open land where the bent grass grows.'

This first settlement was founded as a clearing in the centre of the Great Forest of Windsor. The forest was first used by the Saxons, and then by the Norman Kings, as a hunting ground – with harassing laws, which carried severe penalties for anyone found poaching or interfering with the animals therein.

The sheer size of the forest necessitated the provision of hunting lodges where the King and his entourage could stop and rest. Binfield was one of these stopping places and the fourteenth-century Stag & Hounds inn may well have been a converted hunting lodge. Queen Elizabeth I is said to have watched the maypole dancing from this building, and also stayed in other houses in the village. But her mythical reputation for sleeping out is well-known. Outside the inn are the remains of an ancient elm tree, said to represent the exact centre of the forest.

Binfield does not have its own entry in the *Domesday Book*, but is mentioned as part of the royal manor of Cookham. The entry reads that a portion of the Cookham lands belonging to Reinbald, the King's chancellor, is in the Forest of Windsor and refers to both Binfield and Sunninghill, where chapels annexed to the minster church at Cookham were administered by priests.

The first named priest at Binfield is Walterus, Presbiter de Benetfield, who occurs in a document dated before 1162. By this date the church had passed into the hands of the Abbey of Cirencester.

The use of the name Benetfield occurs after 1160, and by 1230 a family had adapted the title when Henry de Benetfield is recorded as holding the manor. Between the

The Stag & Hounds, Binfield, with the ancient elm said to be the centre of Windsor Forest.

thirteenth and fifteenth centuries, the manor was part of the dowry of the Queens of England, who also had interests in Cookham. A smaller manor in Binfield was held by John de La Beche in 1328. For his manor house and 120 acres of land, he paid 4*s* and 8*d* rent every three weeks to the manor of Cookham.

The parish Church of All Saints dates back to the fourteenth century and perhaps replaced an earlier wooden chapel. There are many large residences in the parish with similar names, including Binfield Court, Binfield Park House, Binfield Lodge, Binfield Manor and Binfield Place. The last named is probably the oldest and dates from the reign of Henry VII, though now much altered and reduced in size. Of the original building, only the eastern wing survives. John Dancastle bought the manor of Binfield from the Crown in 1585 and thereafter created a dynasty which continued until 1754. It would seem that there were at least four John Dancastles, the third having a memorial placed in the church at his death in 1680. The fourth John resided in the manor house during the reign of George I and was a great friend of the Binfield poet Alexander Pope.

Pope was born in 1688, two months before the Glorious Revolution, and came to Binfield in 1700 when his father, who had a sizeable fortune, bought a twenty-acre estate in which to retire and pursue his favourite hobby of gardening. This estate was later known as 'Popes Wood'.

Pope was a Catholic, and as such was excluded from public careers, that being the climate of the time. Nevertheless, he was fortunate in gaining the friendship of Sir Edward Trumbull, who lived in the nearby Easthampstead Park, and with whom he took daily rides in Windsor Forest.

The home of Alexander Pope, the poet who lived in Binfield.

In 1712 he published his celebrated poem, 'The Rape of the Lock', which caused a minor scandal in Berkshire. He left Binfield in 1716, but not before completing 'From Windsor Forest', which expounded the beauties of the area. Pope died in 1744, having lived through the reigns of five monarchs.

The first eminent person known to have spent his honeymoon in Binfield was William Pitt, who bought the manor from the last John Dancastle in 1754. Pitt was the first Earl of Chatham and was later to be known as William Pitt the Elder, a statesman, Prime Minister and Lord Privy Seal of England. Pitt has perhaps never been equalled as an orator or a leader of Parliament. In addition to these attributes, he was a great minister of war and a master of world strategy. He was the type of man to use in the time of a national crisis, and steered Britain through the Seven Years War, when the British were sheep without a shepherd. 'I know that I can save this country and that no one else can,' he had boasted. This he did, and won the trust of the middle and lower classes who referred to him as the 'Great Commoner'.

It was Pitt who built the house that we know as Binfield Manor today, and landscaped the gardens and lakes to suit his own tastes. It is said that he spent £36,000 on the mansion, which was completed in 1754 for his new wife, Hester, the only daughter of Richard Grenville of Wotton Hall, Buckinghamshire. Pitt had three sons and two daughters, the second son being William Pitt the Younger, a great statesmen like his father. Pitt the Elder died in 1778, at which time the family sold the house and moved elsewhere.

The manor house was sold by Pitt's nephew to Buckworth Herne, who passed the title to William Coxe. The next owner was George, Lord Kinnaird, who bought

Binfield Church, *c.* 1961.

it from Coxe in 1787 for £10,000, a bargain even by eighteenth-century standards. While Lord Kinnaird held the manor, the historian and controversialist, Catherine Macauley Graham, moved into the parish after completing the first volume of *Mrs Macauley's History of England*. Married twice, Mrs Graham was described by Mary Shelley as 'a woman of the greatest abilities that this country has ever produced, endowed with a sound judgement and writing with sober energy and argumentative closeness.' She believed that all men were equal and her belief naturally included women.

In 1796, the manor passed to Claud Russell. During his occupancy, Binfield had a famous visitor in the person of the artist John Constable, who also spent part of his honeymoon in the village. Constable had married Maria Bicknell at St Martin's Church and they started their honeymoon in Weymouth with his friend, the Reverend John Fisher, who had performed the wedding ceremony. After a six-week stay, he moved to Binfield where he lodged with his friend's parents-in-law, the Reverend William Cookson and his wife. Cookson was rector of Binfield from 1804 until 1821, and had been tutor to William Pitt the Younger.

During his stay at Binfield, Constable made two sketches of the church. At this time his talent still remained unrecognised, and even after completing *The Hay Wain* in 1821 his earnings were still meagre. In 1822 he painted Salisbury Cathedral for his friend John Fisher, who was then a bishop. This painting too was unappreciated and it was not until after his death that the public acknowledged him as a classic painter.

Claud Russell continued to hold Binfield Manor during the reign of George IV. The rector of Binfield during this time was Henry Dyson Gabell, a distinguished man who had been headmaster of Winchester School. Changes had taken place in the parish with the enclosure of Windsor Forest, which commenced in 1817.

In 1822, William Cobbett visited Binfield and stopped for breakfast at the Stag & Hounds. Cobbett was an essayist, politician and agriculturalist born in Farnham, Surrey. In 1762, he undertook a series of political tours, traversing England on horseback and taking in the flavour of cities, towns and villages. On his rides he travelled hundreds of miles, the accounts of which he regularly printed in his paper, *Cobbett's Evening Post*. These essays were later published in a collected form in 1830 as *Rural Rides*, which ranks today as a minor classic. A leading journalist concerned in the movement for Parliamentary reform, Cobbett tended not to pull any punches when describing conditions in late Georgian England. While on his travels, he drank no wines or spirits and ate no vegetables, contenting himself mainly with bread, milk and water.

During the Victorian era, the manor of Binfield passed from Claud Russell to Sir F. Wilder, whose widow sold it to Mr Kinnersley. In 1896, the manor house and sixty acres were sold to Lord Arthur Hill. It changed hands again in 1907 when it was purchased by Lestocq Erskine.

Today Binfield retains its identity as a country village, serving also as a dormitory area for the ever-growing town of Bracknell. It has seen its share of eminent people, and will no doubt see more in the future when they take their place in the history books.

Eccentric people will often go to extravagant lengths to satisfy their own pleasures, and none more so than Marshal Henry Seymour Conway, who 200 years ago arranged for a megalithic monument to be dismantled in Jersey and transported up the Thames by barge to his estate in Wargrave, where it was re-erected. Marshal Conway was an important military man in Britain and had purchased the Park Place estate in 1752. He had a passion for follies and built several in the grounds of the estate over the years. There was a Chinese house, a brick-faced flint tower, a shell grotto, and two obelisks for a start. To this he added the spire of St Brides Church, which stood on a specially-built pediment. Between 1781 and 1786, he erected a substantial edifice known as Conway's Bridge, which now carries the Wargrave to Henley Road. Viewed from the river, the bridge is impressive and is said to have been built of rocks from fourteen different countries, with other pieces from the ruins of Reading Abbey.

The story behind the megalithic monument began in 1785 in St Helier, Jersey. It was discovered by the military by Fort Regent on Mont de La Ville, an eminence of 181ft above sea level on the east side of the town. A paper read to the Society of Antiquaries in January 1787 describes it as:

Temple Coombe, the Neolithic passage grave at Wargrave.

> Fifty-six feet in circumference, composed of forty-five large stones, measuring 7ft in height, 6ft in breadth, 4ft in thickness, containing four perfect cells and one destroyed. The supposed entrance which may be called a subterranean passage, faces the east and measures 15ft in length.

In March 1787, Marshal Conway, then Governor of Jersey, wrote of the discovery to the Earl of Leicester and stated that:

> The present temple remained entirely covered with earth till the summer of 1785; having the appearance of a large barrow or tumulus, in which form I had constantly seen it when in the island. It then happened that the colonel of the St Helier militia wanted to level the ground for the exercise of the corps. The workmen soon struck on the stones, and the temple thus discovered was afterwards cleared as it now stands.
>
> By the very imperfect accounts we have of the history and antiquities of the island, there is reason to think it has been very particularly the feat of the Druids and their worship. Mr Bindextre, who wrote tracts of the affairs of Jersey, and died in the year 1691, says that there were existing in that small island no less than fifty of these Druid temples.

During the eighteenth century many monuments, like Stonehenge, were wrongly considered to be the work of the Druids. The Jersey monument would nowadays be termed a passage grave or communal burial chamber and attributed to the Neolithic culture of around 2000 BC. The original monument would have been roofed and covered with earth, taking on the appearance of a large mound with the passage as its entrance.

The tomb may well have proved an obstacle on the Fort Regent parade ground as later in 1781 the people of Jersey decided to move it. To show their admiration for the governor, the States of Jersey offered the entire monument to Marshal Conway as a gift to take back to his estate in England.

Duly, in 1788, the circle was dismantled stone by stone, loaded into a barge, and transported to Wargrave, where it was re-erected to its original plan on a slope overlooking the Thames. The whole costly exercise would now be considered an archaeological disaster, but no doubt satisfied the whim of an avid folly collector.

After the death of Marshal Conway, the Park Place estate was split up, and about 1850 a yellow-brick mansion was built in the parish of Wargrave and named Temple Coombe after the monument which stood in its grounds. At a later date this building was demolished and a modern house bearing the same name erected on the site.

When the Noble family put the estate up for auction in April 1946, there were fears for the safety of the monument and Reading Museum carried out a survey of the tomb. It was found that some of the Jersey granite had been replaced with sarsen stones which outcrop on the Marlborough Downs. Obviously at some period one of the owners had decided to remodel the monument, while retaining the basic plan.

In 1962, as a result of the leasing for development of the Temple Coombe estate, there were renewed fears for the temple, although by this time it was protected by a clause in the lease. The circle was once more examined and several fallen stones re-erected by a working party from the Berkshire Archaeological Society.

The monument is now on private property, and is as impressive today as that day in 1788 when it was first erected, although it is debatable whether it should ever have been moved in the first place. The faded marble plaque carries the following inscription in French, 'This ancient Druid's temple was discovered on the 12 August 1785, on the mountains of St Helier in the Island of Jersey. It was presented by the people to His Excellency, General Conway, their Governor.'

It is perhaps a shame that the monument cannot easily be viewed by the public, but it is pleasing to know that it is being preserved for posterity.

Other titles published by The History Press

Maidenhead Voices

CHRISSY ROSENTHAL AND ANN DANKS

This absorbing book brings together the personal recollections of people who have witnessed many of the changes that have taken place in Maidenhead during the last century. Complemented by 100 photographs taken from treasured family albums and archive material from the Maidenhead Heritage Centre, *Maidenhead Voices* recalls the daily life of the local townspeople, whose experiences and reminiscences are recorded here in their own words.

978 0 7524 3290 8

Berkshire Byways

PETER DAVIES

'If I were to list my principal hobbies', says author Peter Davies, 'they would include gawping: not idly or uselessly, but with awe.' Berkshire has plenty to be awestruck about. First there is the ancient trackway of the Ridgeway: is there a more splendid walk in the country? Part history, part guide, Berkshire Byways takes us on an appealing and insightful journey around this often overlooked county.

978 0 7509 4960 6

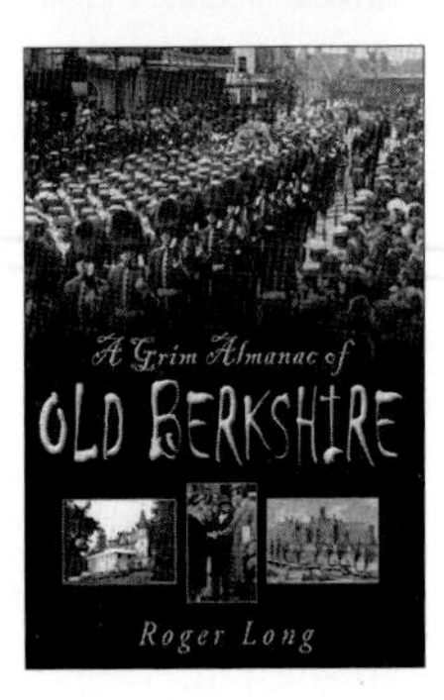

A Grim Almanac of Old Berkshire

ROGER LONG

Roger Long has investigated archives for evidence of the darker side of Berkshire life anc brings his findings together in this day-by-day guide. A Grim Almanac of Old Berkshire includes tales of murder, smuggling, strange deaths, bodysnatching, bizarre disasters and more. If you have ever wondered about what nasty goings-on occurred in the Berkshire of yesteryear, then look no further – it's all here. But do you have the stomach for it?

978 0 7509 3511 1

The Changing Thames

BRIAN EADE

In this long-awaited book, Brian Eade returns to his beloved Thames for a third time. In a collection of over 200 photographs he compares scenes from days gone by with contemporary views, all the way from the river's source in Gloucestershire to Teddington Lock. Images of houses and pubs, lock-keeper's cottages and industrial buildings are juxtaposed with photographs of wharfs, weirs and locks. This affectionate portrait of the Thames will delight river people and visitors alike.

978 0 7509 4779 4